Music Practice MAKEOVER

Strategies to
Make Practice with Your Music Student as Painless and Efficient as Possible

Christine E. Goodner

BROOKSIDE

Music Practice Makeover: Strategies to Make Practice with Your Music Student as Painless and Efficient as Possible

First edition, February 2022

BROOKSIDE

Brookside Suzuki Strings, LLC
Hillsboro, OR
christinegoodner.com

Editing: Shayla Raquel, shaylaraquel.com
Cover Design & Interior Formatting: Melinda Martin, melindamartin.me

ISBN: 978-0-9991192-6-6 (print)
ISBN: 978-0-9991192-7-3 (EPUB)

To my younger self:

There is nothing wrong with you.
There is nothing wrong with your children.
Practicing together isn't easy,
but there are ways to make it easier.
You're not the only one struggling.
It's going to be worth it.

Contents

Preface

Welcome to the music practice makeover. You might be reading this because music practice in your house is a challenge. You might be new to practice with your child and looking for ways to make it successful right from the start. Or maybe you're a teacher looking for ways to support the students and families you work with.

I'm guessing if you picked this book up to read, practice isn't already perfect. You realize it's a lifelong journey to learn to work with children and support them in the best way possible. That's certainly how I've come to see it.

There are always new research findings and fresh ideas, and it's easy to feel anxious and worry if there is something we could be doing better. In fact, between the time I write this and the time you read it, there will be new ideas and research out in the world and more to learn.

But that's okay. This book isn't about having to know everything. I hope we all, myself included, keep learning all the time and never stop. But in the meantime, today, how do we work together? How do we practice the best we can, right now?

A good friend recently told me many resources describe the latest research about practice, but what parents need most is to hear about the dynamics of the practice relationship. I couldn't agree more.

Whether that's between a parent and child, a grandparent and child, an aunt or uncle and child, or a practice mentor and child, music practice is where we improve our skills. It takes a healthy, working relationship to do it well. Through the process, we learn to work with each other and with ourselves.

When it's time to practice, we take a big breath, come into the practice room, and make the music. We train our brains and muscles to do the work. We put in the time and build perseverance.

All the practice strategies in the world are only good if we can make them work *for us*. There will be moments of joy and ease as well as challenging and frustrating moments along the way, and we will go through them together.

This is how we're going to discuss practice in this book. How do we navigate our relationships with each other and with ourselves?

This is where the magic happens. And I can't wait to talk all about it.

Before we go on, I want to acknowledge that not every student has an adult who can practice with them, or access to music lessons at all for that matter.

As an educator, I'm passionate about expanding music education so more students have access to the joy and benefits of music in their lives.

I'm also passionate about expanding our definition of *practice coach* beyond the language of mothers and parents alone, so you'll see me using the terms *parent*, *practice coach*, and *mentor* interchangeably.

I hope as a community we can look to expand who has access to music education. I hope we also expand what a practice coach or mentor relationship might look like.

Having trusted adults who help us in the practice room is such a wonderful privilege. I know I will be forever grateful to my own parents and mentors for what they have given me.

I can't wait to share more with you that you can apply to your journey. Let's go!

INTRODUCTION

What I Learned the Hard Way

I STARTED MY TEACHER TRAINING ABOUT THE SAME TIME I BEGAN TO practice with my oldest daughter. But our journey started even before that.

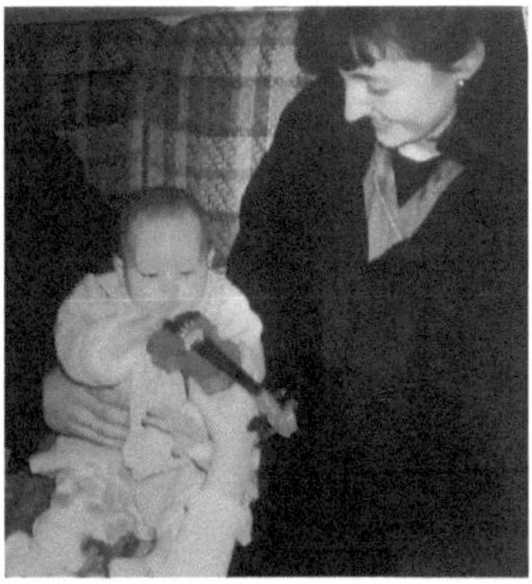

I recently found a picture of my daughter and me when she was an infant. In it, I'm holding up a teeny violin next to her, a one-sixty-fourth size, or about the size of a protein bar. At the time, she was way too young to start holding, much less playing the violin. She had yet to master standing and feeding herself. But the look I'm giving her in this picture gives me goose bumps because it so well sums up how I felt seeing her with that tiny violin.

I imagined the wonderful times we would have together with music. I imagined smiles shared. I pictured hugs and warm moments. All wrapped up in that tiny violin. I imagined we'd bond, spend time together, and get to know one another. I imagined her life would be better with music in it. I could already feel the immense pleasure of helping make that happen. All these images flashed in front of me at that moment, captured in that picture.

And when this daughter was four years old, we did start her on the violin. I was a young mom, money was tight, and so I became the teacher and parent. I had the help of my dad, who was my wonderful practice parent. He acted as an additional practice support—a relief pitcher, so to speak.

And my daughter and I *did* have wonderful moments through music. There were hugs and smiles. Her life was shaped and formed through music in ways I could never have imagined. And we did get to know each other through the process in a special way.

But if I had only known the ups and downs ahead of us.

If I had known that my idealistic ways and my desire to be a "good teacher and parent" and do things the "right way" would clash so strongly with this child who would have indescribable determination . . . I don't think I would have the same look of joy on my face.

It was hard. We had power struggles. There were tears from both of us on more than one occasion.

And if I'm really honest, I blamed myself. Clearly, I was doing something wrong. Maybe my child was not cut out for this kind of thing. I really wondered if it was all worth it. And there was no worse feeling since I spent my days convincing other people it definitely *was* worth it. I wasn't just failing. I was a fraud of some kind.

And so, I did what I always do when overwhelmed: I took a step back. I went back to my textbooks from my early childhood education degree. I stepped back and decided no one else had to know I was "breaking all the rules," but I was going to put the *right* way to practice aside for a moment and find out what this particular child needed to practice effectively.

The daily battle of wills was too much, and I decided not to let practice become a daily fight anymore. I gave more ownership to her earlier than I would have recommended at the time. And we learned the hard, slow way how to practice together.

It would be years later before there were online discussion groups where parents could discuss practice challenges and ideas. And a few years ago, when I published my first blog post called "Confessions of a Suzuki Parent" about how I had struggled to practice with my own children, I felt sick to my stomach when I hit PUBLISH.

My colleagues would know I was a fraud. I was clearly the only one who was a teacher having these issues, at least in my mind. My list of fears went on and on. But just as I was sure I was outing myself, I was also just as sure there were other parents out there who needed to hear they weren't the only ones struggling. They needed to hear that other parents had the same issues with practice too. Maybe you're one of those parents.

So I hit PUBLISH.

And that's really when I felt, for the first time, that actually what we went through, both my daughters and I, was surprisingly quite normal. I actually wasn't alone, not even close. Many people, including countless teachers, have reached out since then to thank me for talking about this topic and helping them feel less alone too.

I've spent the years since those early struggles to practice with both my daughters gathering research, forming strategies, and sharing creative and useful ideas with other teachers and parents. I've made it my life's mission to share them and try to help ease the way for other adults like myself working to help young children practice.

I wrote a book all about what I wish I had known when starting out with my own children called *Beyond the Music Lesson: Habits of Successful Suzuki Families*, and it started opening up lots of conversations with other teachers and parents about how to help students thrive in music lessons. It also pointed out to me that we need to talk about what practice at home really looks like. Sometimes what is actually part of the typical ups and downs about learning to practice feels frustrating and slow. I realized that the topic of music practice needed a lot more attention so that the process could be demystified and the whole range of experiences that people might have could be seen as normal.

This book is the result of my own research, best practices I have found helpful, and many conversations with an amazing community of teachers and parents that surrounds me.

It shares some of my favorite strategies and the best information I know at this moment to help you set your child up for better practice sessions from the start. Or if you need it, help you figure out how to get things back on track.

Here's how it came about:

In 2018, I published a workbook about practice called *Positive Practice: 5 Ways to Help Your Child Develop a Love of Music*. It's meant to be a quick read for busy parents, with helpful information and space for reflection as well as prompts to take action.

Since then, I have heard great things from many people about how the resource has helped with home practice. A teacher recently told me when she held parent-teacher conferences with her studio families for the first time, nearly all the concerns parents brought up about their struggles with practice were addressed in this framework, which helped her feel confident about supporting them. I also heard that a gymnastics teacher used it to talk to classes about practice in the context of the sport.

And while I heard from many people who used the workbook and found it helpful, I also realized that many more people could use the information better with the concepts fleshed out a bit more.

I started to do that by offering many small, online workshops, giving more ideas for the concepts I shared about practice and holding discussions to help address specific examples. In these workshops, parents and teachers discussed the ideas in-depth. They help one another by adding their own experiences, and over time, I got to see the impact my practice framework had. This only got me more excited about how I might be able to help those whose practice needed a makeover.

I love seeing the light-bulb moments and hearing how practice was turned around over the course of a week. This is exactly what I wish had been available to help me when I was practicing with my daughters. It's exactly the gift I want to be able to give to you.

I'm excited now to be putting that workshop content into this book so more people, like you, can get the extra support for home practice. I want more teachers to feel that they can point families to a resource that really helps in a crisis or when setting up new practice habits.

I hope this becomes a resource with dog-eared pages and notes in the margins. I hope it's a resource you can easily refer to when you need the extra support.

I recommend reading this book all the way through if you're reading for the first time. But I understand you may want to jump to topics you feel you need right away. However you use this book, I hope it encourages you and helps give practice in your house a makeover for the better.

CHAPTER ONE

Productive and Positive Practice

I SPEND A LOT OF TIME AND ENERGY WRITING AND SPEAKING ABOUT positive practice. Many families would not describe their practice sessions in those terms. When practice sessions are filled with conflict, or when we can't tell if we're getting better and making progress, it can be very discouraging. But music practice doesn't have to be like this all the time. If you relate to this description, I hope you will come to realize that there is hope of creating a more positive practice routine.

But what does positive practice really mean? Is having positive practice sessions an unrealistic ideal? Some people may think so.

I think it depends on how you define it. I am under no illusions that everyone's practice sessions will be upbeat and happy 100 percent of the time when practicing an instrument. Reading this book will not suddenly mean there aren't challenges that come up. Our children likely won't be grinning from ear to ear each time they enter or leave the practice room. Some students may have that experience, and that's wonderful, but I'm guessing if that's already you, you wouldn't be reading this book. I'm going to focus my attention on what to do if that's *not* the case.

An Honest Look at Practice

Practice is hard work. Sometimes it feels tedious. We can make rapid progress sometimes and, during other times, feel like nothing is happening. In the challenging moments, we may wonder if we're just wasting time or if we're doing it all wrong. And what you may not realize is that sometimes that's even true for the *professionals*. Recently, I've been following the violinist Hilary Hahn as she shared one hundred days in a row of her own practice sessions on social media.

What I found so refreshing is that some days she had effective, satisfying practice. Other times she only fit in a few minutes or admitted feeling frustrated that she was having a less focused practice day.

How refreshing to see that even world-class musicians have ups and downs when they practice. In fact, this is what practice is all about. We can't control if practice on a certain day will feel productive or not; all we can do is show up and give it our best. Entrepreneur, speaker, and best-selling author Seth Godin gives such a good perspective on this that applies to music practice and so much more: "Anyone who has ever learned to walk, talk, or ride a bike has gained these skills without full assurance that the effort will lead to success on any given day. But only the effort is under our control. The results are not."[1]

What I love about Hilary Hahn sharing her process so publicly was being able to see her approach to these ups and downs, which seemed to be simply acknowledging the day for what it was and trying again tomorrow. That acknowledgment of reality is precisely what I would prescribe for young students.

If a world-class professional has her ups and downs, certainly we can make space to normalize it for our children and students.

Unlike some other activities our children may participate in, when it comes to learning an instrument, our children may love certain aspects of playing but still find the discipline of individual practice sessions a challenge. I can't emphasize how normal it is to love one or more aspects of playing our instrument—like performing, taking lessons, or making music with peers—but resisting the hard work we do individually in daily practice.

Even if we enjoy the challenge of overcoming what's hard and the problem-solving involved and find it invigorating, it's still work, and it still takes discipline. Some of us love that, and some of us resist it. Some days we can't wait to dig in and get started. Other days we may think of every excuse we possibly can to avoid it. There are professional musicians who fall on both sides of that spectrum. So it makes sense that there are students who do too.

Our relationship with practice has more to do with our relationship with repetitive and disciplined tasks in our lives than our love of our instrument or music itself. As we move forward, that's an important distinction.

Positive Practice Defined

My definition of *positive practice* includes the following:

- Working together productively with mutual respect.
- Having a feeling of accomplishment when we leave the practice room.
- Building the habit of practice so it becomes part of our routine.
- Learning something, or improving it.

Music practice involves deep focus, including a huge range of emotions that are all part of the process. It can be intense, and that's fine, as long as it's intense in a productive, healthy way.

We are allowed to, and probably will, get frustrated. We are humans working at a skill that takes a considerable level of focus and attention to detail. There will be ups and downs. There will be good days and not-so-good days. If the practice relationship breaks down, the important thing is to talk it out and repair our relationship by connecting, apologizing if needed, and coming up with new strategies together.

I always want my own students to know that it's okay not to want to practice. I think it's counterproductive to consider this "bad" or inappropriate behavior in some way. I don't always want to practice. I still need to do it and I still need to come into the practice room treating those around me with respect and not yelling, for example. But it's perfectly human and normal not to want to practice.

Simply acknowledging this can help us get past that feeling of "Ugh! I don't want to!" and then move on to get our practice in anyway. Child development experts recommend naming feelings to help young children process them, rather than talking them out of these feelings, and I think that's a helpful strategy to adopt for children and adults alike. We will discuss strategies for getting practice started more easily later in this book.

Whether we are the ones practicing or we're working to practice music with young children, what we *do* need to have is empathy. We can employ what experts call *cognitive and compassionate empathy,* where we try to understand how our child might be feeling, and we can take steps to help.[2] Students can greatly benefit from having a trusted adult helping them do this as they learn to practice their instrument.

It's my experience that the more we allow for the natural ups and downs of practice and accept they are a part of the process, the more we can take them in stride and enjoy the moments of connection, inspiration, celebration, and joy that are also a big part of the process.

Throughout this book, we will be exploring these different aspects of positive practice. We'll also be talking about ways you can make positive changes in your family's practice life.

Why Is It Important to Think about Positive Practice?

Consistent and effective practice is a huge part of being successful on an instrument. Unlike other activities our children might participate in, the real work that moves us forward and develops our skill doesn't only happen at the lesson or with the teacher but in the everyday practice that happens at home.

Great teachers are important. Our teachers will explain the concepts and ideas that get assigned for follow-through so we can develop them through practice.

Our teacher gives us a road map to follow for practice. They help us have light-bulb moments when complex concepts start to make sense. They help break down complex skills and help us make things easier. They help us understand the repetition that will be needed to make complicated concepts and skills easier for us. Our teachers help keep us on track toward improving our skills and meeting our goals. They help us prevent bad habits, or help us catch and correct them early, so they don't get in the way of our progress.

I can't emphasize the importance of great teachers enough. But only the student can put in the time, work, and repetitions to learn and incorporate what their teacher has taught them into their playing. As teachers, we don't have a magic wand to give you the skills you need instantly. Believe me, I wish I did! Through repetition and attention to detail during the daily and weekly work, we learn and incorporate our new knowledge and skills.

The Role of Practice Coach

I like to think of the adults supporting young people in practice, be it parents, grandparents, siblings, or other mentors, as *practice coaches* or *practice partners*. The relationship will be different between the student and teacher versus the student and practice coach. This is especially true for parents practicing with their own children. There are complicated and layered relationships involved. The key is to focus on coaching students through the work involved and helping support them in the process of practice.

If you are practicing with a young student, your role is invaluable. Students often need support to make effective practice happen at home. We can't expect still-developing brains and bodies to understand and function the same as adult professionals or any adult for that matter. The younger the student, the more I, as a teacher, am relying on support from a practice partner to make practice happen productively.

If practice at home is negative, filled with conflict, or lacks progress, it is so much harder for a music student to be successful long term. It certainly doesn't make it easier to become self-motivated and love playing our instrument when practice is unpleasant on a daily basis. There are many stories of students overcoming adversity or being extremely self-driven on their own. However, it's my belief that if we want each child to have the chance to learn music at a high level, we have to move past a sink-or-swim mentality and actually teach the skills that students need to succeed.

We can define that success in many ways for the purposes of this book. It's easy to agree that the result of a professional musician is a success. From my perspective, success is also developing a lifelong love of music. It's developing enough skills on the instrument to enjoy playing it, to the best of their ability. Even if a child doesn't play their instrument for the rest of their lives, I consider it a success if a student has an appreciation for music and the instrument from their time in music lessons with me.

Our children may come away with many life skills from their time practicing and learning music that stick with them for their whole lives. Learning to focus, learning to break down big challenges in small pieces, and learning to stick with it when it's not easy are just some of the skills I see develop in students over time. Who doesn't want that for their children?

Big-Picture Thinking

When I speak to groups of parents in workshops, I often ask: What do you want your child to have gained from this process ten years from now—whether they still play their instrument or not?

We will often end up with fifteen to twenty answers written on the board (and could likely just talk about that topic alone for a full hour). Typically, there are one or two answers about musical skills or technique, and then the rest of the answers are things like: persistence, discipline, love of music, confidence, learning to problem-solve, and the opportunities and communities their child will get to be a part of through music.

I always find this so interesting because as parents and caregivers, many of us often feel pressure for our children to develop certain skills at certain times. We feel the urge to compare their progress or to "keep up" with other students around us.

However, when we really think about the big picture, this is not what our most important goals are for our children long term. There is a disconnect between the two.

Few parents would say, "I want my child to learn these skills the fastest of anyone else," if they also had to sacrifice these other big-picture goals.

I encourage you to take a few minutes and brainstorm a list for yourself. What *do* you want your child to gain from studying their instrument, whether or not they play it for the rest of their lives?

Keeping our big-picture goals in mind can get us through many challenging or frustrating times. Practice didn't go well today? Ten years from now, we want our children to know that they shouldn't get discouraged and give up when something is hard or doesn't come easy right away. We want them to know if they can't solve a problem on their own, there are resources they can find and mentors they can connect with to help them. We can model this long-term thinking and hold on to the long-term vision when our child can't, or when they aren't developmentally able to yet.

Instead of feeling frustrated with our children, or ourselves, I invite us all to zoom farther out. What really matters? We may need to break down our practice into smaller chunks. We may need new strategies. We may need to take some pressure off and focus on what is going well, then come back to the challenge tomorrow.

We may need to do more research as the practice coach about how to inject some creativity and fun into practice. We may need to really observe our children to see what engages or motivates them.

One of my favorite concepts that helps reframe our goals in practice is from author Dr. Benjamin Hardy in his book *Willpower Doesn't Work.* He writes that you can design an environment to meet your goals by "creating conditions that make your success inevitable."[3]

What would it look like if we did that in our music practice? Under what conditions can we help the child in front of us be successful? Under what conditions can we improve our practice sessions and enjoy the process?

The answers to this question are never one-size-fits-all. While there are some general principles that all the students in my studio use to practice effectively, the secret formula for them individually, that makes practice easier for them, is almost never exactly the same for any two students. It may not even be the same for an individual student from one day to the next.

Here is the reality: the students we teach and practice with may or may not become professional musicians. However, adults in almost every profession that I can think of, musician or not, need the skills of not giving up when things are hard. They need to know how to work with themselves through challenges. They need to learn to work with their strengths and get help in areas where they do not excel. Learning these skills through our instrument is invaluable.

It's worth developing these skills whether or not we will become professional musicians. It's also very normal for practice to be a challenge, especially for beginners. It's not just the students who find practice easy right from the start who will go on to become accomplished musicians, or adults who still have music in their lives. I absolutely believe every child would benefit from a music education. It doesn't have to look the same for everyone to have value. With new information, resources, and strategies, we can make music practice work better for our child's needs.

What if It's a Struggle?

Through my work, I have many conversations with families asking if they should continue lessons since it's hard for their child to practice. Many people wonder if this is a sign that their child doesn't really like to play their instrument. And I totally understand where they are coming from because I asked myself that very same question.

Here's what I have concluded after wrestling with this dilemma for two decades. Many times, a student who struggles with practice loves something about playing their instrument. They may love performing or playing in groups. They may love their lesson or their orchestra experience. Often, the challenge is that they are still learning *how* to practice.

A student might be coming up against something that isn't easy for them for the first time in their lives. Or they may feel many conflicting feelings when they love and dislike something so strongly at the very same time. That's very confusing, especially when we are young.

As the parent, I saw part of my role as helping my children remember what they loved about being involved in music. I tried to get better at letting them feel the hard things and not talk them out of their moments of frustration. I shared how I sometimes felt frustrated or that progress was slower than I wanted when practicing too.

You don't have to be a musician to empathize. Perhaps you're studying a new language, learning a new process at work, or training for an athletic event. You can likely recall some time in your life when you were working hard to learn something new. "I've felt like that before too!" is a powerful way to connect. We know why it's worth it to keep going when there are parts we love or rewards at the end of a struggle. Our children don't have that experience or wisdom yet. We can help hold that part for them.

Most parents want their child to learn the rewards of sticking with something challenging that has a great reward at the end. Music can absolutely be like that. The trick is, as nice as that sounds, it's during the challenge and the wanting to give up but sticking it out anyway that we learn that skill. Through the struggles, we build the character traits and life skills that many of us are after when we encourage our children to learn an instrument.

Often, the biggest challenge is not about the instrument itself. It's about learning to do things that are hard, that take time and effort. An instrument is a great way to learn to work through those feelings. We will come up against them somewhere in life. Perhaps it will be somewhere else like math, writing, or studying for tests. We may come up against obstacles and challenges in sports or athletic endeavors. Certainly, there are other ways to learn this than music, but practicing an instrument is one great way to do it.

When I was wrestling with big questions like this, and especially with that feeling of anxiety about making the right decisions for my children, I could always come back to these big-picture ideas. I want them to love music. I want them to learn to focus and work hard. I want them to have amazing friendships and experiences with peers through the community that music offers. I want them to feel that magical feeling when a beautiful piece of music is made in collaboration with others that can't even be properly described in words.

Those are the things I am after.

Many situations and circumstances can cause us to question our commitment to this process:

- "Today was hard."
- "A skill is taking longer than I think it should."
- "My patience is wearing thin."
- "Someone else we know seems to be going 'faster.'"
- "My child has trouble continuing on when frustrated."

Those situations sometimes felt overwhelming to me in the moment.

Now, with two kids in their twenties, and with daily practice long behind us, I can tell you all how glad I am that I didn't let those things deter us. I can tell you things got easier. It was worth it.

CHAPTER TWO

Practice Misconceptions

I was diagnosed as a young adult with inattentive type ADHD. I always knew my brain worked differently, but it was a revelation to me that all these things I struggled with, was even lectured for, or told were flaws in my character were actually a legitimate difference in how my brain worked.

I only knew to go in for screening when a parent came to my studio saying that their former teacher wouldn't work with them anymore and asked if I was willing to look over a list of symptoms to see if I would. I got quite emotional when I read the list. On that list were all the things I beat myself up for my whole life in black and white, with a name.

When I was growing up, it was commonly believed girls didn't suffer from ADHD, and my parents didn't even know this was a possibility. I often struggled to focus and to turn in assignments on time, even though it was clear I was not struggling to understand things. I am quite sure it was frustrating to practice with me or see that I had a lot of ability but struggled to practice effectively.

I share all this because when I was diagnosed, my doctor told me that I had accomplished what I had in school, despite my ADHD, likely because of the fact that I had been in music lessons all of my childhood. Studying music had given me structure and taught me to work with my strengths. The structure and discipline

I learned through music had taught me skills I needed, even though they hadn't come easy.

Music was wonderful for me for its own sake. I loved making it, sharing it, and all the social opportunities attached to it. Music also changed my life because it gave me other skills I needed. While I wasn't born with an ability to focus well, through music I learned how to focus well enough to reach high levels of playing—and *that* transferred to other areas of my life too.

And then I started to practice with my own children.

One of the things that caused me the most sleepless nights when they were young was falling into the trap of comparing ourselves to others. Sometimes I compared our practices to an imaginary ideal that I now don't think actually existed.

I put a lot of pressure on myself to have an "ideal" practice. I was sometimes crushed by the weight of all the things our practice "should" be and "should" look like. When I questioned if we should keep going or what was wrong with us, I think it most often happened in this context:

- Practice *should* be easier.
- My child *should* focus more easily.
- She *should* be motivated on her own if she likes this.
- Our practice *should* be X number of minutes long.
- My child *should* be on a more advanced piece or playing at a higher level.
- This *should* be fun, not frustrating.
- Everyone else is making this work, so why can't we?

What I've Learned

Here's the reality I learned: While practice may look fairly similar for advanced players and professionals, practice with young children probably will look like many different things. It may be short bursts of hard work with planned breaks. Young children may need to move often between their time holding still and focusing. Practice may look like work disguised as silly, creative tactics. It's often a joint effort between practice coach and student. Music practice changes over time and gradually becomes closer to what we picture when we think of practice.

Some young students can focus for a long time and have a more grown-up, advanced practice approach from the start. That's great too! However, if our process looks a little messier and unorthodox at the start, that doesn't mean we won't get there. It doesn't mean we're doing it wrong.

In my opinion from decades of teaching, from an early childhood education perspective, and as a parent, I think we're badly mistaken if we insist the process of learning an instrument has to look the same for everyone.

I believe many students have not continued in music, or were not given the opportunity to, because their approach looked different at the beginning stages.

As parents, we may struggle with questions like:

- How much should we push our children?
- What is appropriate to expect for their age?
- How much of the ownership over practice should be ours versus theirs?

I have been giving a lot of thought recently to this outward pressure to practice in a prescribed way and the pressure we sometimes put on ourselves to do it the way we *should.*

I think of the ways I beat myself up as the practice coach with my own daughters because I had a number of misconceptions about what practice should look like for young children. This was true even with my training as a teacher.

I want to share some of these misconceptions with you in case you're falling into this comparison trap too. We don't need to compare ourselves to others; we're all on our own journey with our own process.

As we talk through these ideas, I want to emphasize that all of these things *can* be true for your child. But from my experience teaching and talking to teachers and parents all over the country and many all over the world, they are not true for everyone, especially when children are very young. My goal is to help us take the pressure off by not pressuring our children or ourselves by these ideals or misconceptions. There is no need.

Myth #1: The Lone, Focused Practicer

Ask the average person what they picture when think of music practice, and usually an image pops in their head of a person standing alone in the middle of a room in front of a music stand intently focused. The image may be a person on the piano bench in front of the piano, or it may involve a stool and a harp, but this is the most common image in my experience.

This probably comes from media images, documentaries of famous musicians, and all sorts of other snapshots we see of professionals. It comes from our own parents who put on kitchen timers for our practice time and hollered from the kitchen at us to get back to it as soon as there was any silence. I'm sure it comes from all sorts of places in our culture.

Sometimes practice does look like the lone, focused practicer. But speaking as a teacher who works with preschoolers and who practiced with my own children, this is not how practice starts for most musicians.

Sometimes practice with preschoolers looks like rolling on the floor, leaving the practice spot for hugs, bursts of dialogue that seem to have nothing to do with the task at hand, and creative and inventive ways to get one more good repetition in on a given day.

This is all so normal and, I would argue, developmentally appropriate. It's easy though to compare this to the image of the lone practicer and feel quite concerned.

- "Does this even count as practice?"
- "Good thing no one else can see what *our* practice is like!"
- "How embarrassing that it takes all this to get a few minutes of practice in."

Parent of the preschool-age student: Please let go of any guilt or shame about this. I promise it's very common.

Perhaps our children are not preschoolers, though. Maybe we allowed for this kind of practice when they were beginners, but they're a bit older now. Let me reassure you that most students I know who go from the roll-on-the-floor mode to focusing for long periods of time do it gradually.

We build focus and motivation over time. Tiny bursts of practice with breaks become slightly longer bursts of practice with breaks. Rolling on the floor is replaced with dragging our feet when transitioning between tasks and so on.

I can't tell you exactly when to expect your child to focus longer during practice. It's highly based on their development and their individual skills for focusing and organizing themselves in life, not just in the practice room. You can notice what focus is like for your child while doing schoolwork or tasks around the house. Can they focus deeply not only on tasks they really want to be doing, but also on those that must be done but take more discipline?

Long periods of focused work can be an end goal. It will certainly be needed to reach the highest levels of performance and achievement. But it's in the late teen years before we can expect it all across the board for students. And then, some students with learning differences, for example ADHD, may always need to have intense bursts of practice spaced out.

Should only the students who have this ability from the youngest ages be allowed to continue with music? Emphatically, I would say no. Just like my own story from earlier in this chapter, we can learn focus and discipline *through* the study of music and the daily practice that comes with it.

Music offers us a way to learn to work with ourselves. It is not a prerequisite to start with all the skills needed to focus and practice well. Focus is built and developed. It can be supported. It needs an environment to thrive and grow in.

We don't have to start out as the lone, focused practicer. In fact, we will save ourselves a lot of frustration and angst if we see what is possible for our individual child as we start and build from there.

Myth #2: The Light Switch

When I give a talk to parents and ask them if they have any questions, two very common issues that come up are focus and motivation. As parents, we wonder why our children are not self-motivated. We wonder why it's so hard for them to get started. We try to figure out what's wrong that these two issues cause so many problems.

There comes a point, later than most parents wish, when a spark is lit in our child to practice and work hard because they are determined to improve or learn a certain skill or piece of music. I love seeing this happen. I also know that it's usually somewhere in the teen years when this happens consistently. Some students have that spark very early. For other students, I've seen it hit late in high school or even college.

One of my favorite quotes about this related to young children comes from my friend and colleague Rachel Ludt: "You can't schedule the focus of a preschooler." It was a light-bulb moment for me to have language to describe what I wanted parents to understand about practice with young beginners.

Focus and motivation can't be flipped on like a light switch, especially for young children. I think over time we learn what we need to transition to a productive practice state and can get ourselves in that mode more quickly. Very young children often will struggle to practice unless we keep their very real needs in mind and pick our timing carefully. Considering when a child *can* focus and working with it, rather than insisting they do focus when their brains and bodies may not be able to cooperate, is a key to success for sure.

Sometimes what we think of as a lack of motivation is something else. Sometimes we have to make sure the conditions are right for our children to get into a focused state. They don't have the life experience yet to know when that is. If families can make practice happen in the morning, that often helps.

Certainly making sure biological needs have been taken care of:

- Are we exhausted?
- Are we hungry or thirsty?
- Do we need a bathroom break?

Young children, even beyond preschool, may have a limited amount of intense focus to give in a twenty-four-hour period. We have to be strategic about scheduling practice if we're going to ask them to learn a complex music instrument as part of that allotment of focus. Saying "Focus! Focus!" does little good in this case. Instead, we are going to time our practice and then teach what *focus* means in bite-size chunks.

The same thing applies for motivation. Motivation is not something that is magically present if we're supposed to be musicians. Musicians find motivation in social outlets for musicmaking, in wanting to achieve something they have seen someone else do, and in wanting to play a certain piece of music, for a few examples. Sometimes very young musicians find motivation in stickers, pieces of candy, or playing concerts for stuffed animals.

Research shows us that when a skill is new and everything about it is hard, this is when rewards help us push through and keep going. In his book *Atomic Habits*, James Clear addresses the fact that we want motivation for our goals and habits to be internal. For example, those of us reading this book likely want our children to practice because they want to improve their skills or because they are motivated by the music itself.

However, young children often can't see that far ahead. What they see in front of them is a lot of hard work. It's hard, if not impossible, for them to see all the exciting payoffs from it yet. "In ten years, you'll be so glad you did all this practice" is not a motivating statement to a young student. It's certainly hard to feel motivated by long-term payoffs when there are many hours, months, and even years ahead of us to get there.

Best-selling author and habits expert James Clear writes: "Early on, it's all sacrifice . . . In the beginning, you need a reason to stay on track. This is why immediate rewards are essential. They keep you excited when the delayed rewards accumulate in the background."[4]

Those immediate rewards of stickers or chocolate chips or high fives from our practice partner are key to keeping us going when everything is new and challenging.

Dr. Rebekah Hanson and I interviewed teens at the advanced chamber music program at the Oregon Suzuki Institute, and all the teens in our panel said they were finally motivated by the music and a sense of accomplishment when they reached an intermediate-advanced level (around Suzuki books four and five). They all said this is when they started to feel like playing the instrument was something they might be good at, and they got past the stage of feeling like everything about this is *hard.*

In my mind, this is a good estimate for the earliest we can expect the self-motivation and motivation to play music for it's own sake to kick in. Of course, your results may vary. Helping create a motivating environment fills the gap until we get there.

Myth #3: The Movie Montage

While staying at home during the pandemic, my husband and I rewatched the '80s movie classic *The Karate Kid.* It brought back some great childhood memories, and I realized just how many times I had watched it with my brothers because I could anticipate each line of dialogue before it started.

There is a famous scene when the star is practicing his crane kicks on the beach. It's a time-lapsed scene with the waves crashing and soothing music playing over the clips of, what we assume, is hours and days of practice. Eventually, in an inspiring climax to the scene, he masters the skill.

There are endless examples of movies when the main character has a struggle of some kind, and then we see the transformation:

scenes of deep practice when the hero endlessly writes their novel, or endlessly practices their crane kicks, or whatever other skill they need.

We see many snippets of hard work that are meant to have taken place over weeks or months or years with nice music over the top and the hero comes out the other side having been transformed.

It's a great device in movies. But I've been thinking that for many of us who didn't grow up studying music, it can give us the wrong idea. No one plays soothing or energetic music over the top of frustrations and meltdowns in the practice room. We have no assurance going in that it's all going to work out okay in the end. There is no way to speed up the constant work that goes into developing our skills.

The montage is great for movies, but it can give us the wrong idea about practice. Practice can feel exciting and fun. It can also feel tedious and frustrating. Our path to mastery and playing to the best of our ability doesn't go in a straight, neat line. It's often messy with ups and downs. We have to trust the process because we don't know the way the story ends for us. All that uncertainty can feel uncomfortable. I think it's important to talk about. I see movies with this plot device and now I always smile to myself and think, *Wouldn't that be nice if music practice had this feature?* Maybe for you it will be a linear, motivating process, but if not, that's okay. This is real life, and most people will have ups and downs, good days and bad.

Myth #4: Practice Looks the Same at All Levels

My sister played varsity soccer and was quite good at it. I was remembering recently that when she started playing in preschool and kindergarten, she participated in what was called "kick-and-chase soccer." It was well named and a bit like herding cats. As a teenager at the time, I found it quite amusing. I'm sure there were parents who had played themselves who found it frustrating to watch.

The beginning soccer players ran the wrong way on the field. They would make goals on the other team's side by accident. Sometimes they would be seen sitting in the field picking dandelions or looking up at the clouds as if they were making snow angels in the grass. It was a bit chaotic and also adorable.

If we compare this type of practice to what my sister's varsity soccer practice looked like in high school, or to what practice looks like for the World Cup soccer team, it has very little in common. They were on a soccer field and had a soccer ball, but really they were just learning what the game was. They were figuring out what it meant to simply be on the field. That the ball went into the goal in the first place. They needed to build the stamina to run back and forth on the grass in a certain, hopefully one day correct, direction. Practice changed a lot over the next couple of years for those young players, but they weren't expected to practice the same way as the women's World Cup team from the start—and a good thing too.

In the same way, young musicians are starting off with their own version of "kick-and-chase" soccer. The practice sessions of beginners may not look very organized. They are just figuring out what it means to come into the practice room and interact with their instrument and their parent. They are learning to focus. They are learning to control muscles they don't use much otherwise. They are learning what it means to interact with a teacher in a lesson and take instruction and so on.

We have to start somewhere. Each semester or year of playing, we will slowly start to look more and more like an advanced player. It's a process.

This doesn't mean we don't teach the skills needed, or don't think about careful, quality practice sessions. But it does mean we don't need to worry if it looks different to practice at the beginner level.

Perhaps we can only get in a few minutes to start with, or it looks less disciplined than we imagined. Comparing the way children practice to elite performers is a sure way to feel inadequate. Your teacher has a path to get you there. You need only to trust the process and work with where your child is at the moment and know you will build on it over time. The chaotic and disorganized beginning practices will eventually take shape into more focused and disciplined work as we build our skills and knowledge about what we are doing.

Have You Been Subscribing to Any of These Myths?

I encourage you to reflect on these practice myths. Have you mistakenly believed any of them? Do any of them seem to apply to your child or someone you know, so you assumed they were true for everyone? I encourage you to look for ways you might be buying in to these myths and notice them around you in things you read and hear people say. It can be helpful to know we can let them go and start to get a more accurate picture of practice that is rooted in reality for our child and those we work with. That will give us a great foundation to build great practice habits from right where we are.

Throughout the rest of this book, we will be discussing what practice really looks like in the beginning and intermediate stages and ways to make your practice sessions work for your child and their individual needs. By thinking about all of this information, it is my hope that you finish this book with a solid plan of how to get started with practice or give your music practice the makeover it needs.

SECTION ONE

The Real-Life Ups and Downs of Home Music Practice

CHAPTER THREE

Supporting Music Practice at Home

Tiana Angus is a violinist, performer, and music educator in Queensland, Australia. She performs and inspires students, and still, practice at home with her own child isn't always easy. She recently told me: "Practice is a challenge, but we keep going because of all that can be learned through music: creativity, joy, a love of music, discipline, the importance of routine, and all of the other life skills that are developing." Her thoughts sum up well both what I experienced practicing with my children, and what I hear from many families who are making practice work in their households.

As we start to discuss what practice looks like behind-the-scenes for many families, I want to share a research project I conducted and presented at the International Research Symposium on Talent Education (IRSTE). IRSTE is a symposium established in 1990 by Margery Aber at the University of Wisconsin–Stevens Point and is "a means to promote research among Suzuki teachers, disseminate research that influences teaching practice, and educate teachers to use research in resolving studio challenges."[1] Over one hundred parents who practiced with their children from across the United States and Canada participated. They were referred to the research through online forums and their own studio teachers. They weren't necessarily students studying in the Suzuki method, but they were parents who practiced regularly with their children.

The participants answered questions about things like:

- Did you have any struggles in home practice, and what were they?
- What is the one thing that makes learning music and practicing work in your house?
- What words of advice would you give to another parent starting out with practice?
- What is the best part about seeing your child learn and practice music?

I wanted to find out what parents would share anonymously when they didn't have to admit to their own teacher what their struggles were. I also wanted to know how common the struggles that I had experienced, and saw the families in my own studio experiencing, were. I wanted to see if what I had learned through trial and error and my own personal research applied to a broader range of students and families.

Participants who answered my questions ranged from parents of preschoolers who were early in their journey of practicing all the way to parents of college students or adults who were reflecting back, and each age group in between.

One of my favorite quotes from a participant, a mom of a now grown violinist, is: "Suzuki parenting was the hardest but most rewarding thing I ever did." This quote is the most accurate description I have ever read about practice with young children.

I think we can say that about parenting too. Period.

The more I talk about this topic with parents and reflect on my own parenting journey, the more I think we could take music out of it completely and say the same thing: "Parenting was the hardest but most rewarding thing I ever did."

Working closely with our children is challenging and all-consuming, but it can be beautiful and affirming all at the same time. We may wonder if we're doing it right. We may lose sleep, hoping our children turn out okay. We may realize we had no idea what we were getting into when we signed up for this wild ride. *And* at the same time, we can feel so grateful and we wouldn't want to have it any other way.

All of these things are true about parenting and helping our children practice while parenting. What makes it hard to get our children to brush their teeth and make their beds also makes it hard to get them to practice, or at least practice effectively. It's easy to lose sight of goals, like developing a love of music or bonding together through music practice when these issues arise.

I recently had the pleasure of interviewing violinist, music school owner, and business coach Rebecca Lane, who shared her own related experience and insights into the kind of help our children often need to make practice happen. She sums it up well: "They won't even brush their teeth properly unless I monitor them, and with practicing, it's very similar. They're not going to eat vegetables, they're not going to brush their teeth, and they're not going to put their shoes away unless I ask them to. We have to be very consistent with these things, and practicing their instrument is no different."

Just as we learn how to build routines and help our children to learn the importance of these daily tasks, such as brushing teeth, spending time supporting our children through their music practice helps build routines and helps our children see the benefits of practice over time. We can help support the learning process and the ups and downs along the way by being there to support them as they learn to practice, learn to be consistent, and learn to play their instrument.

How Do We Start if We Need a Practice Makeover?

When practice is hard and we feel frustrated by lack of progress or conflict in the practice room, it's easy to get overwhelmed. It may be hard to know where to start to make practice more effective and productive.

When music practice was challenging with my own children, if someone had asked me to describe which part of practice was the hardest, I don't think I could have answered them. It wasn't one clear thing. It all felt hard. Everything.

It was like a messy room packed with clutter. If someone asks which part is the messiest, it's hard to say because it's all messy. When things are overwhelming during home practice sessions, it's easy to feel the same way. You may feel like it's impossible to decide what to do first to make things better, and that can make it hard to start making positive changes.

Over the past twenty years of parenting, teaching, and talking with hundreds, if not thousands, of parents, this theme comes up often: "Help! Everything about this is hard." I've thought a lot about how to help untangle that and find somewhere to start making things better, and I hope some of what I learned will help you as well.

The good news is there are many ways to practice and great resources to support you. There are many approaches to making practice work. You don't have to find the magical, perfect way to practice. Instead, we're going to discuss ideas so you have many options to choose from as you learn to make practice work in your house for your unique child.

The first thing to know is you are not alone. There are absolutely ways to turn things around in the practice room. If you're looking for how to start, it helps to find a little thread to pull as we begin unraveling what feels like a big, jumbled mess in the practice room.

Often, when we find ways to make small, positive changes, everything feels more hopeful and manageable.

If you are just starting out, these ideas will help you as you create positive habits from the start. These habits can help make practice as positive and productive as possible right away and may help you avoid some unnecessary struggles. I like what Suzuki violin teacher and parent Abigail Peterson says about this:

> For me, music is almost as important as any other school subject. I also think it brings this beauty to your life that you can't get from other things. And that goes for my students too.
>
> Maybe they'll be performers or teachers, or maybe music will play some role in their career, but in most cases, they're not going to and that's fine because there are so many beautiful ways to use music in life. It could be playing in a community group or playing in a church, or whatever role it takes.
>
> In our home, we prioritize music pretty much on the same level as any other school subject, but we don't forget the true gift that it is, either. There are a lot of tools we can use to ensure it's not a negative experience. That's why I care so much about helping parents navigate practice (as a teacher): having their child take music lessons and make it a positive thing.

This is our goal, and as you read further and look for solutions for practice in your own house, I am going to ask you to keep this important reminder in front of you: There are many ways to practice things, but you only have one relationship with your child.

It's a wonderful gift to spend quality time together through music, and putting that relationship first will help us find solutions and make progress in a healthy, supportive way. If we see that something about practice is causing undue stress to our child or the practice relationship, it's always wise to step back and evaluate if the strategy is working and to know there are likely other approaches if it's not.

As a teacher, I always want to know about situations causing stress in practice because it's often a signal to me that we need to break down practice tasks into smaller, manageable chunks. I don't want families in my studio to tough it out or to have practices that are full of tears or meltdowns. If something is not working, we can find creative solutions together.

Finding strategies that reduce overwhelm and help us learn more easily and effectively is a great place to start when we want to inspire motivation and a love of music. If something is getting in the way of all that, let's address it and make things easier.

CHAPTER FOUR

Real Talk about Practice

You may be reading this as the parent of a new music student looking for ways to avoid and reduce struggles. Or maybe you've been practicing with your child for a while. You want to make it easier to practice together and reduce the conflict that sometimes comes up during practice sessions.

It's probably no surprise to you that practicing music is hard work. Likewise, most people realize when they become a parent, there will be highs and lows as they help their children learn new skills. When we combine those two realities, that's where some of the challenges we encounter in the practice room come from.

Either way, it's important to share the parts of learning an instrument that are positive and helping us make progress. It's also important to support one another and talk openly about the challenges that come up along the way. When we sign up for music lessons, we are committing to help support children through the process of learning a complicated musical instrument. This can look very different depending on the age of our child, and we will address this more in-depth in Chapter Twenty.

For now, let's remember that in order to help students practice effectively, we often need to support them during the ups and downs in the practice room. Feelings like frustration, joy, and everything in between are part of the process. What we may not have anticipated when signing up for music lessons is that our children often need our help to navigate these feelings. Add to that reality that we may be parents who feel tired, overwhelmed, or short on patience for any number of very valid reasons on a given practice day, and this combination can naturally create some conflict and emotions to run high in the practice room.

I don't want to dwell on the negative, but I do want to acknowledge that you may be experiencing some of this and let you know how normal it is. You're not doing anything wrong. We're all human. We're going to talk about how to avoid getting bogged down in these struggles as we strive to improve our practice session together. We want to acknowledge that it's normal so we can work to improve things at the same time.

Parent-Reported Challenges

When I first started practicing with my daughters many years ago, I really thought we were the only ones having the practice struggles we had. I have since learned so much about effective practice and how many families experience the same thing, but it felt very isolating at the time. Feeling alone added another layer of stress to our practice sessions as I tried to figure out what I was doing wrong all those years ago.

Every time I talk to groups of parents, many people come up to me to tell me they've felt this way too. If we can normalize talking about the messy parts of the process, I think we can all let out a big deep breath and put more energy into solution-finding rather than feeling like we're doing something wrong, or like we have to pretend things are all going smoothly when they aren't.

Not everyone will have the same struggles or all of the struggles we discuss here. Take what applies to you, and if you can't relate, please realize there is someone else out there who needs to read it. You can skim on through, or perhaps come back to it later if it crops up and you need it in the future.

I hope you'll come away from this section of the book feeling like you have a better understanding of what to expect in practice, new strategies you can use, and that you don't have to spend any more time worrying if something is wrong with anyone in your household if music practice isn't easy.

Help! I Have to Remind My Child to Practice

Your child might love arts and crafts. They might love building with blocks or other materials. They might love to read. They likely start many of these activities spontaneously without anyone telling them.

So why then, if they really want to learn how to play an instrument, don't they start spontaneously practicing their instrument too?

I get this question so often: When will my child start to initiate practice?

Or: Why doesn't my child get started practicing on their own?

First, some students do just go practice on their own. That is the reality for some families, to be sure. But after raising two children of my own and teaching for two decades, I will tell you this is often the exception and not the rule.

I've recently been interviewing teachers and professional musicians for a podcast series, and each interview so far I have asked this question: "Do you remember liking to practice when you were younger?" The responses often include laughter and an enthusiastic no; so far, no one has said yes. But over time, these professionals learned to enjoy the benefits of practice, and most of them said it was when they went to college to get a performance degree that they really started to enjoy it.

I recently interviewed violinist, educator, and activist Calida Jones and asked her what she remembered about liking practice growing up. She said: "I did not enjoy my home practice. However, I really liked practicing my orchestra music. I was in the DC youth orchestra program, and I would come home after four hours of sectionals and orchestra and practice my part. I loved it. I could hear the harmonies. I could hear what was happening in those pieces and I loved playing them. There were certain sections that I would just play over and over again. But my technique stuff, absolutely not."

Learning how to practice is its own separate skill from learning the technique of our instrument. Many professional musicians will tell you, just like Calida Jones, they loved certain parts of playing instruments growing up, but the discipline of it was a challenge for them too.

Of course, over time, with experience and wisdom, musicians learn that it's the challenging parts of practice that help them build their skills. The hard work in the practice room is the thing that helps us improve. Understanding this makes it easier to dig into what we need to practice and get to work.

Professional musicians know they will be glad they did practice. They may not love the act of practice, but they love having finished their practice session for the day. They know the benefit, and that makes it easier to get started, which can be a real challenge for students. The pros likely have a routine to get themselves in practice mode. Plus, they have the experience to know why it's worth it.

I encourage you to think about how you feel before starting any activity you know you want to do but drag your feet to get started at the same time. Maybe it's lacing up shoes before an exercise session or starting up the computer before a work project that takes deep focus.

For many young musicians, practice is something they do because their teacher and parent require it. Oftentimes, young students cannot understand yet what the long-term payoffs will be from all this hard work. They may need more immediate rewards and celebrations along the way to keep their motivation going. They may need more help transitioning into practice sessions. All of this is why we don't see many students initiating their own practice until they've been playing their instrument for a while and have the ability to understand the long-term benefits.

Internal Motivation Will Eventually Kick In

While it may take many elaborate routines, rewards, and reminders at first to get a practice routine going, this won't last forever. As students continue with music and start to develop more practice skills and long-term thinking abilities, practice often starts to feel more motivating. Students want to practice for the music learning and skill building itself.

A shift happens where it starts to feel really rewarding to focus on learning something challenging and having the skills to make it easier to play a piece of music or a technical skill on our instrument. Until then, we, the adults, can hold on to the long-term thinking and motivation for young music students so we don't all lose sight of them.

Practicing music takes planning, organization, and high-level thinking skills. These skills and abilities develop well into our teens and early twenties within the brain's prefrontal cortex and are often referred to as executive functioning skills.[1] While skills on our instrument can develop at an advanced level earlier, these executive functioning skills may not have developed fully yet at earlier ages.

What Are Executive Functioning Skills Exactly?

For more information on how to understand executive functioning skills and how they apply to music practice, I reached out to educator Emily Hawe. Emily is a certified teacher and executive function coach who describes executive functions skills as your brain's air traffic control tower. "Your brain is bombarded with information every second. Your executive function skills (which don't fully develop until age twenty-five) are responsible for deciding how to prioritize, remember, process, and organize that information." She recommends thinking of the following as your "control tower team": impulse control, emotional control, sustained attention, task initiation, planning and prioritizing, organization, time management, goal-directed persistence, flexible thinking, and working memory.

As you can see from this description, many of the skills that are necessary for effective music practice involve executive functioning and may need our support even through the teen years.

My advice is always to pay attention to your child's, or teen's, overall approach to tasks that involve organization, planning, and follow-through. Do they always make their bed, turn in paperwork on time, and keep themselves on a schedule and organized from day to day? For young children, the answer is very likely no. They likely need support and guidance as they learn to do these types of tasks. For our teens who do these tasks independently in other areas of life outside the practice room, it may be possible for them to take more responsibility for managing their practice sessions.

Often, parents chuckle when I ask if their child does tasks like this independently because their child needs many reminders, and perhaps someone to be right there in the room with them, to get some of that done. If your child needs help with these organizational tasks outside the practice room, they likely need help to get started and to organize their practice sessions.

As parents, we often go through a process of helping our child with these tasks and then slowly, over time, giving them more and more responsibility to do it alone.

Violin teacher Daniela Gongora shares her perspective about practice for her son like this: "My son is able to clear the dinner table and load and start the dishwasher all by himself. He began doing this as an activity with his dad from the age of four. It took three years until he was able to master the loading and starting of the dishwasher, so I think we will give ourselves that same timeline toward unsupervised practicing."

There are likely many examples in your own life where you can think about how you used to do something for your child and then gradually gave over the ownership of that task to them on their own. If you are heavily involved in helping with music practice at the start, the process feels very similar. Knowing we will help build skills over time takes some of the pressure off. It also will set students up to learn how to practice with your assistance over time, which is a huge benefit to them.

This challenge with getting started in the practice room is often not about loving music or having motivation. It can be more about how students manage tasks that take organization and planning and have multiple steps involved instead. A parent in one of my workshops told me, "I consider myself my daughter's prefrontal cortex until hers has developed more fully." I love that way of thinking! We can help our children be successful by standing in and supporting these skills as they develop.

Practice Is Its Own Skill

Remember, practice is its own skill, and it develops separately from our instrumental skills. We tend to lump all the different aspects of practice together when talking about it. However, it's important to remember that learning to play the instrument and learning how to practice are two very different things. It's perfectly normal to like one and not the other. It's normal to feel like one is something we look forward to, and the other is something we want to avoid.

We can tell our child is getting frustrated during practice in a number of ways. They might be very obvious and dramatic or very subtle. Parents report some of the following as signs of frustration in their children:

- tension in their body or hands
- foot stomping
- audible sounds of frustration
- slumping to the floor or sitting down
- asking when practice is over
- playing wrong notes or purposefully, aggressively doing so out of frustration
- emotionally shutting down and becoming unresponsive or giving one-word answers
- full-blown tears or meltdowns

It's always wise to start to learn the cues for our individual child so that if frustration is creeping in, we can try to change tactics or give a short break to regroup before they are completely overwhelmed. This can be a sign we need to break down the assignment into something smaller or easier, even if it seemed manageable yesterday.

If there is practice frustration happening at your house, it can be really helpful to step back and think about what is causing the most frustration. Is it a technical skill on the instrument, or a skill related to learning how to practice in general?

When we are struggling with technical skills, perhaps we need to spend more time focused on building technique in our practice each day. We may need to ask the teacher if they have other ideas about supporting those skills in practice. Very likely, we need more repetitions of the assignments we already have.

Maybe we need creative ideas to help our child tolerate the many, careful repetitions in a row needed to improve our technique.

If, however, the trouble is our child taking the initiative in getting started or being more organized about their approach to practice, the real issue is developing our practice skills, not instrument skills. We may be expecting too much too soon. We can often find ways to offer some extra support. We can and should consider how old our child is and how well they organize other parts of their life.

Thinking about practice as two separate sets of skills—technical skills and the skills for how to practice well—helps us determine ways to help and support our child through any challenges that arise. We'll talk all about supporting practice in the next section of the book.

The Ups and Downs of Practice

When I give parent talks, I often show a picture of a roller coaster by photographer Chris Slupski. It shows a mom and child having a blast with their arms in the air, a parent and child looking relaxed and peaceful, and then in the front, the child's face looks quite unhappy.

I picture her thinking, *I do not like this! How do I get off?* I think this image sums up what it can feel like to be a parent in the practice room. We may feel all of those things at one time or another. Maybe over a year, or even all within one practice session. Our child is likely to be feeling them too.

Sometimes, everything about practice and learning music feels effortless, and we feel like we've got it all figured out. Then sometimes, our kids go through a new set of developmental changes, and we're not even sure what we know anymore.

Sometimes, we see our children struggle or get overwhelmed by frustration and challenges, and we worry about the adults they will grow up to be.

Other times, we watch our children from afar in a performance or in a group class or interacting with their teacher, and we get a glimpse of the adults they're going to be. Then we can see very clearly it will be okay. We see they are growing into wonderful humans right before our eyes.

We're likely to experience all of this through music practice. The ups and downs are part of the process. The concern and celebration are part of parenting, in my experience. It may give us sleepless nights and gray hairs, but hopefully also many joyful moments to celebrate too.

ACTION STEPS

- Remember that the prefrontal cortex, which helps us plan and organize practice, is still developing until early adulthood.

- Keep in mind that practice skills and technical skills on our instrument are two different things.

- Remind yourself how normal it is to still need to give reminders for practice.

- Think about what other skills your child has developed over time with your support; learning to practice may be very similar.

CHAPTER FIVE

The True Story of What It's like to Practice at Home with Young Children

In the 2018 research I conducted, I knew even before seeing any results that practicing with children was often a challenge. However, as the results came in and I began to look at the actual numbers and data, I was blown away at just how common it actually was. Most strikingly, every single participant reported having some kind of struggle with practice.

While I wish no one had to struggle, it's nice to know it's part of the process for everyone at some point. When I tell parents this is hard for everyone, I'm not just trying to make them feel better. At least in my research, it's actually true and many experts agree. I love what music educator Susan Beth Barak shared with me about this:

> The way we humans are wired, **there is no learning without struggle** and making "mistakes," which are both natural and needed steps in the process of skill development. Once you recognize that there are no shortcuts around the hardware of our biology, you can truly **celebrate the struggle as a sign and site of progress and growth!** While you may never exactly enjoy the sensation of struggle, you can learn to take satisfaction and pride in knowing

> that sticking with the process means **you can do hard things**!
>
> —Susan Beth Barak, MEd, OCELT, RMT, RYT-300

Learning how to stick with the process, work through these struggles, and realize we can do hard things is exactly what we will be talking about throughout this book. First, let's talk about what some of those challenges might be.

Some parents in my research said they went through a single struggle at the beginning of their child's lessons. Then, they worked through it, and things were great after that.

Other parents said they overcame struggles, and each time they did, a new one would come up. They would tackle the next one and then the next. That was their process over and over again.

I would imagine many of you reading this can relate. Maybe you even have multiple children whose experiences vary, and it's very different with each child.

There Are Many Positives Too

I loved hearing the things people said they loved about practicing with their children at home and what made it worthwhile. The range of answers covered themes, such as seeing instrument skills develop, watching their children grow as humans, and realizing the relationship with their child had developed more deeply in the practice room.

Here is some of what parents anonymously shared:

- "Getting to have a better relationship with him. It has really strengthened our bond. It has brought us so much closer!"

- "Watching them struggle and then overcoming it with hard work and effort."
- "Watching him develop musically and emotionally."
- "It's a special time for us. I have learned a lot about negotiating both our personalities to develop the habit. I've gone from seeing it as a chore to treasuring it as the best part of our day."

Common Struggles

There were a few main themes that came out when parents shared what their specific struggles in the practice room were. Some of them were not surprising to me, but others were more unexpected. What I've come to realize since first doing this research, and now having shared it with many groups of teachers and parents, is that there are struggles that are easy to talk about, and others we are only going to share with someone we trust. We may want to be out of earshot of our child, whom we don't want to embarrass, at the very least.

I've come to realize how vital it is to have honest, open communication between teachers and practice coaches for this to happen. Our teacher may have great solutions to help or great resources to point us to, but we need to be able to share what we're struggling with to ever find out about them.

The first time I spoke about this research with parents and teachers at a conference, it was my theory that sometimes teachers don't hear some of these struggles talked about so openly because parents are embarrassed to share them with us. It certainly seems easier to simply say we're too busy to practice and not get into the details.

As I was walking in the hallways of the convention center after my talk, a parent came up and shared that she wasn't embarrassed to admit any of the struggles they had in practice at her house. But, she told me, there wasn't a format for her to do that with her teacher without her child present, making her uncomfortable to bring it up.

As teachers, I think this feedback is a good reminder to think about how we are providing opportunities for conversations like this for families. I hope we can all think about how to open up communication in a way that helps us support the practice process and make things easier. We want parents to have opportunities to ask for help or advice that is not in earshot of their child so they can feel comfortable and talk openly.

To help facilitate these conversations, I want to share the top three struggles parents reported to me in my research. I now use this as a way to start meaningful discussions and hope you can too.

Time

As a teacher, the practice struggle or challenge I hear most often from families is they don't have time to practice. Overscheduling is a real issue for many families. I was expecting this to be the largest percentage of answers. What surprised me was that "having enough time" was only the biggest struggle for 25 percent of those who answered. Participants were asked to pick one answer, so maybe time would have shown up for everyone if they could pick more than one option. We can assume it's true that most families feel pressed for time, but for many people, it's not the most significant issue they are facing.

In casual conversations in my own studio, time is talked about the most as a challenge. However, when we have parent-teacher conferences or more one-on-one conversations, that's where I tend to hear about the other challenges, which we'll discuss next.

I've come to realize that saying "We didn't have time" may also be covering things like:

- "Work was stressful, and I didn't have the energy or patience this week to practice."
- "Someone in the family was sick."
- "We spent the time we use for practice arguing about getting started instead."
- "We went into the practice room to practice but just couldn't get anything productive done."

We may not want or need to share those details in a quick conversation at the start of the lesson. When I want to help make practice easier, though, it's helpful to think about what is truly a time issue versus something deeper or more complicated.

The Parent Role

About one-third of the parents in my research reported that the parent role in practice was their biggest struggle (32 percent, to be exact). Some parents reported that it was hard to fit everything they were assigned into a practice session.

Others said it was hard to stay patient through the daily practice on an ongoing basis. Many parents said that having the energy for music practice with their child every single day was an issue.

It's important to note that this was the biggest struggle reported by this group of parents. As a teacher, I think it's important to remember that many parents, and caregivers we work with, are feeling this way. If we never hear about it, it could be that they don't feel comfortable bringing it up.

Maybe as a practice partner, until seeing it in writing like this, you couldn't quite articulate what it is about your role that is challenging. It's so important to have outlets to talk about these challenges with other adults helping their children with practice. There's nothing more reassuring than hearing, "I feel that way too!" This is exactly why I am writing this book. I hope you come away from reading it feeling like you are much more equipped to support your child's music practice by the time you've finished reading.

Student Behavior

How children act during practice sessions was the third biggest challenge reported by parents. Twenty-four percent of parents said this was the biggest challenge for them. Some parents reported that their child flat out refused to get started, that they had meltdowns or a strong reaction to feedback during practice (even positive feedback), and others said their child wasn't able to focus on the tasks assigned.

I think this is the most challenging category in a way because we, as the practice partners, have the least control over this particular challenge. We can tweak our schedules to allow for more practice or simplify our schedules. We can work on our own skills and find resources that make our role easier. We can't, however, control our child's behavior.

It's ultimately up to the child to decide to practice. They may be tired, stressed, hungry, or distracted, along with many other possibilities. There are many strategies we can find to make practice less stressful and to build a cooperative relationship so we can have an influence, but we can't make this part of practice go better until we understand more about our child's needs.

In my own training as a teacher, the language was used that the parent's job was to "recreate the lesson at home." I know that teachers asking parents to come to lessons want them to see how assignments and tasks are done and then guide their child through those same activities at home.

It took me a long time to realize how careful we need to be about this idea of recreating the lesson at home. What we really want is to complete the practice tasks carefully and make them easier. If we think we can recreate the interactions between our child and their teacher, we're going to be frustrated to see resistance to the task, to our feedback, and to the focus involved. We might have even seen our child do those things successfully with their teacher.

It's also important to note that things like refusing to get started, noncompliance, or trouble focusing might not be about learning to behave at all. New research on physiology and the brain suggests that many behaviors that used to be chalked up to a need for self-control are really a symptom of overwhelm and a child spending more energy to try to restore calm and reduce their stress levels than they have available to them.

In his great resource, *Self-Reg: How to Help Your Child (and You) Break the Stress Cycle and Successfully Engage with Life*, Dr. Stuart Shanker writes:

> Once you can distinguish between misbehavior and stress behavior, you find yourself better able to pause and reflect when he (your child) does something you find disturbing, rather than reacting automatically . . . Instead of reacting in a way that only adds to the stress and causes the child to burn even more energy you can help the child to calm, restore equilibrium, and recover.[1]

If you find that the typical advice for addressing your child's behavior in practice is not helping your child, I can't recommend this book enough. You can use it as a place to start and follow up with additional resources as necessary. As the saying goes, often our child isn't giving us a hard time—they are *having* a hard time.

Research Recap

Talking about our challenges and seeing that we're not the only ones having them is so important. Normalizing the fact that practice with our children sometimes feels hard can take the pressure off and feel like a relief to many parents and caregivers. Looking for signs of stress and frustration and addressing them when we want to see different behavior in the practice room is key.

For teachers, it's easy to talk only about the technical side of practice. After all, we are working with students to learn to play an instrument. We likely didn't take specific training on how to help support these practice relationships effectively.

However, the fact that 56 percent of parents who answered my questions found either their role or their child's behavior in practice a challenge tells me that we need to address the relationships involved in practice too. It's crucial to understand how to practice and how to navigate the challenges that come along with working together in practice sessions. This is an important part of our plan to help students succeed.

We need to be prepared for when these challenges show up in home practice. Then we can talk about them and find solutions together. We can point parents to useful resources and see that they get the support they need.

As parents and practice partners, we're not asking robots to unemotionally go through the motions of practice. We're living full lives. We're human. Unless we homeschool, practice with our children may be the most intensively we are working with them on learning skills day to day. There is so much to learn about how to practice effectively and how to work with our individual child.

We can start by reminding ourselves that this kind of work with our children is both hard but rewarding. And then we can roll up our sleeves and try to make it better for everyone involved.

ACTION STEPS

- Reflect on which of the practice struggles mentioned in this chapter you might be experiencing.
- Did you notice that any of the struggles mentioned in this chapter used to be hard at your house but have gotten easier? Consider sharing what helped you next time you're talking with other parents about the ups and downs of practice.
- How can you establish ways to have more open communication, between parents and teachers, about the good and challenging parts of practice?
- How can we reframe behavior in the practice room and think about the stress levels of our child so we can help them stay as calm and focused as possible?

CHAPTER SIX

Building Great Habits from the Start

WHAT IF YOU HAVEN'T STARTED PRACTICING YET? MAYBE YOU'RE NEW to all this and are looking for ways to make practice go as smoothly as possible. How can you prevent some of the aforementioned conflicts from the start?

From firsthand experience, I can tell you that you can do everything "right" and still have practice struggles. In my research, 100 percent of the families surveyed had struggles. I think that's important to carry forward with us. There are likely to be great times and challenging times, but we can do what we can to make it easier along the way.

Some of the questions we have to navigate are:

- How do we get everything done in a day?
- Is there a way to practice more effectively?
- How do we find time in our busy lives to make this a daily routine?
- How do we get our children to cooperate with us (especially when we know something is good for them, and they want to avoid it at all costs)?
- How do we stay patient and keep in mind what they can handle at their age and stage of development?

- How do we know our child is actually enjoying or benefiting from music?
- How do we balance learning the instrument with other interests?
- How do we help our child stay or get motivated?
- How can we make this process fun?

We Are Embarking on an Endurance Event

It's important as we start out to know it's going to be rewarding and wonderful in many ways, but it's also going to be hard. I don't say this to scare you off or discourage you. However, I do think it's unkind to think we're going to go on the equivalent of a light stroll but take you on a strenuous hike or to summit a mountain.

If you know you're signing up for an endurance event, you're going to put on different shoes and bring different supplies with you. You're going to put more thought into what you eat the day before and you're going to drink lots of water so your body has the energy and hydration it needs. You're likely to be more prepared.

Learning an instrument is a complex process. It takes daily practice over many years to play at a high level. We need to be aware of what is involved in setting out the project in front of us with the preparation we need.

Your teacher will explain their expectations to you as you get started. It's also beneficial to hear from other parents who have made music practice work for their children and learn what works best. There are also many great resources to guide you, including reading this book.

Whenever I hit frustration or uncertainty in my own parenting journey, I tried to make a practice of reflection and stepping back and gathering more information to guide me. This was true for music studies, academics, and social situations my children were navigating.

When I was a newer teacher, I used to talk to new families in my studio and share primarily all the wonderful benefits of music. I wanted them to be convinced of why signing up for music lessons would benefit their own child and their family. I wanted them to see why it was worth it and how their child would develop a love of music. But after a couple of decades of teaching, my approach has changed.

I still believe all of those things are absolutely true, and I weave them into what I share at the start. But I realized I wasn't helping anyone by only sharing what was easy. I was painting a picture of all the positives and leaving out the fact that it might be challenging too.

If we think again about signing up for an endurance event, we might envision the feeling we'll have crossing the finish line or summiting the peak, and it can keep us going. It may be that feeling of accomplishment that we are signing up to have. However, we likely also know there are going to be challenges. There will be places along the way where motivation wanes or where it takes a real commitment to keep going. There will be sore muscles and exhaustion. We may question if we should keep going or question why we decided to start in the first place.

Another comparison we could consider is learning a new language as an adult. Experts say that it takes anywhere from 600 to 2,200 hours to learn a language, depending on the language.[1] That can be daunting to think about. There will be moments when we feel we're making progress and moments when it feels like we may be a beginner forever until we reach the point of mastery. Even if we have learned a lot, it can seem like there is so much further to go.

If we have an ambitious goal like an endurance event, learning a new language, or learning to play an instrument at a high level, we are going to need a system of support around us. We will need to find resources to help us, to schedule time to practice and study or train, and to keep reminding ourselves why we are putting in all this effort for a long-term goal.

If we combine those two analogies, we have a healthy respect for what we're committing to. One of my mentors shared that she asks families to commit to ten years of studying their instrument before starting lessons. She wants to make sure they are very committed to the process and realize what a long-term commitment it is to play at a high level.

With all of these activities we are discussing, the fun is in the challenge, in the accomplishment of what we learn, and the opportunities and memories we make from what we learn. There are moments when they certainly won't feel fun; they will just feel like plain hard work. These same things are true of practice.

That's what I want to make sure you know as a parent. There is nothing wrong with you or your child if music practice feels hard. It's supposed to be hard. We are learning complex skills, and they take a tremendous amount of dedication and effort to master them. As a parent, we will need to help our child work through all of that, and that also takes a huge amount of dedication and effort.

We can combine that with a vision of where we are going, and all the beautiful parts of learning music can keep us going when we need extra motivation. Remembering the wonderful moments ahead and the parts of the process we do love can get us through the hard moments when the work required feels daunting or unappealing. If we only talk about the good parts of learning music, it's like sending someone off on a strenuous hike in flip-flops. We won't be prepared or set up to be successful.

Start with the Vision

I encourage you to take some time to think about *why* you have signed up your child for music lessons. When I'm leading a workshop, I often ask parents to reflect on this question: "Ten to fifteen years from now, what do you hope your child has gained as a result of learning their instrument?"

Even if your child no longer plays their current instrument that far into the future, and whether or not they become a professional musician, there is so much to be gained through the process. I encourage you to make a list of what that is for you.

Here are some reasons I often hear:

- Perseverance
- Patience or delayed gratification
- Discipline
- Developing a love of music
- Creativity
- Breaking down problems into small, manageable steps
- A willingness to try new things
- Resilience
- Organizational skills
- Appreciating music for life

I encourage you to take a few moments to think about which of these is true for you. You may be able to think of other things you hope your child gains from their music studies and add them to your own list. I find it really helpful to write them down and keep them somewhere to look at them again in the future. You could keep them in your practice notebook, a notes app on your phone, or another spot you can easily access.

When you have a rough week of practice or even a rough couple of months, pull out this list and remind yourself why your family is doing this. You could glance through it for a minute before each practice for perspective. When we feel like learning a new language, training for an endurance event, or learning our instrument is going too slowly, or we feel frustrated by the process, that's when we especially need to remind ourselves why we're doing it. We need to remind ourselves what our goals are beyond today's practice session or this week's lesson.

Children all learn at different rates, and progress can vary over time. Your teacher can help you with specifics about how to practice that technical skill you want to improve on, how to improve your tone, or whatever skill it is that you're working on at the moment. It will take daily, ongoing work to make these challenging skills easier.

It's important to think about what skills we are developing or are improving in addition to technical skills. These things, specifically many on the list we just read, are the ones our children take with them into other areas of life.

They are often the things we hope our child gains, no matter what ends up being the outcome of their instrumental studies. It can be helpful to remember what goals we have when we're away from the instrument. Practice and our music lessons are helping us develop them, and it's important to notice them along the way.

Seeing we've made progress can be so motivating, and seeing our children develop life skills that will carry them forward no matter how long they play or what profession they choose was so satisfying to me as a parent. Balancing out the technical skills, practice skills, and human skills that we are gaining helps give a more holistic approach as we work with and support our children in their studies.

Preventing Problems before They Start

While it may be impossible to prevent any kind of struggle in our music practice, there is much we can do to avoid common problems and sources of conflict. We can learn from research how children learn and from the experience of others who have done this before us. If you're just getting started, you have a wonderful opportunity to set things up well right from the start.

If you are not new to practicing music in your home and you see areas where you wish you could back up and have a do-over, you're not alone. I personally learned all of this the hard way. It is not too late. We'll talk more specifically about how to turn things around in future chapters.

Setting Up Positive Practice Routines

There are four ways I think we can set things up for success right from the start:

1. Setting up a healthy learning environment
2. Helping make the discipline involved more tolerable for your child
3. Creating a routine
4. Understanding what works for your child, especially for their age and stage of development.

Let's break these down one by one.

Setting Up the Learning Environment

When planting a seed in the garden, conditions around us have to be good for growth to happen and for a seed to sprout. Forget to add water or remove access to sunlight, for example, and growth may be very small or nonexistent.

Our young musicians need the right conditions and environment in which to thrive and grow as well.

Learning music is for our child, and ultimately our child has to has to be invested in the process. It takes active engagement on their part to learn to play well. To carry our seed analogy forward, we can't force a seed to grow.

However, we, the adults, have the power to create an environment for learning. We can influence many factors that will set up our children for success. We will do this in part by learning about how our child learns and what motivates them as we spend time together in the practice room.

I love thinking about how Dr. Benjamin Hardy's quote, on conditions that make success inevitable, applies to us in practice. What conditions help a particular plant grow? Some need direct sunlight, while others need shade. Some need lots of water, and some will not thrive if you overwater them.

Of course, our children don't come with instructions about what they need, but we get to learn along the way. We get to learn how to work with them successfully and ultimately help them learn to work with themselves.

Location

Finding a location to hold practice sessions is a great first step. For very young children, this involves finding a spot to practice with the least number of distractions possible. Some people will have access to a practice room, which is wonderful. Many others may set up a practice corner in a multipurpose room or transform an area for practice before each session. It's important to think through when we will practice and what will be the best location in our home so that focused work can happen.

In our modern times, if this is also the space you'll use for any online lessons or music classes, important considerations include being close to a reliable Wi-Fi connection and extra attention to lighting and space for a camera.

In my experience, spending lots of time gathering materials can get in the way of effective practice. Our young child may only have a few focused minutes to give to practice as we get started. If we spend those precious minutes gathering needed supplies from all around the house, we might use valuable practice time.

I recommend that you have a practice bag, shelf, or drawer where you can keep your materials together. Think through what you will need: your practice notebook, perhaps a stool or foot chart, a pencil, and any other materials you are using in practice sessions. Everything together in our practice location makes it much less frustrating to get started and keep going.

The Emotional Environment

Experts recommend reading to young children while they're cuddled in your lap long before they can understand what you are reading to them. In part, this exposes them to a rich vocabulary that aids speech development. Still, it also creates future readers, because children come to associate reading with love and closeness to a caregiver they love and are connected to.

I would argue we want the same emotional environment to surround young beginners learning a musical instrument. Maybe the tasks on the instrument are not yet easy, but students spend a few minutes each day interacting with their music assignments in a warm, loving environment and can come to associate music practice with one-on-one time, encouragement, and connection with adults in their life who love and care for them.

Creating a positive environment, full of encouragement, where we point out what's going well and help make the hard work of practice fun is a must for our children. I want to remind you that my definition of positive practice allows for all emotions to come up but is also one in which we treat each other with respect. We focus on making progress, no matter how small, and we encourage our child's attempts and the effort they are putting in.

Frustration is likely to come up. Strong feelings and days when it's hard to focus will come up. We are still there, helping our children navigate through it and understand that it's okay if it feels challenging and frustrating. Remind them: we can try again tomorrow. It's the same thing I have to tell myself now when I have a frustrating day of practice. Our children don't yet have the perspective to tell themselves these things, but they will learn as we guide them through it.

Help Make the Discipline Involved More Tolerable

As we have already discussed, learning how to practice is a skill. Often, students love to play their instrument but don't love to practice. Of course, some students just take to this right away. A student I worked with comes to mind whose parents had to make a rule of no violin at 5:00 a.m. because if she woke up early, she would go right to the violin and try to work on playing something. And this was at four years old. It was wonderful enthusiasm—just not when everyone else is trying to sleep!

If I could bottle up that enthusiasm and determination and give it to everyone, I would. If this sounds like your child, you may not need to read this section. For the rest of us, it's important to know that this, at least in my experience as a teacher, is not the norm for everyone. For the rest of us, enthusiasm and discipline can be cultivated in other ways.

For many, the early stages of learning an instrument can be challenging. Until the internal drive kicks in, often in the middle or high school years, practice time can feel like plain old hard work. We want to get to the fun part of playing, but the amount of focus, effort, and dedication it takes to get there can feel daunting. Many young children especially need some help and support to develop those skills.

There eventually comes a lesson with each student when I see them start to repeat and practice carefully over and over until it gets easier right in front of me. It's always an exciting moment for me because I can tell they are starting to understand how and why to practice. They are starting to be driven to improve because they want the music to sound a certain way. Quite often, I see this happen in middle or high school.

What do we do at the beginning when this discovery hasn't been made yet? We know we're not just making life difficult by repeating something ten-plus times. It's perfectly normal for our child to resist doing it daily at first. As both a parent and a teacher, my best recommendation is to make the repetitions more fun, or at least more palatable.

A Note about School Music Programs

In my area, most of our local schools do not have a strings program. A few have opportunities for band. I think students who have orchestra or band built into their school day have such an advantage. Often, the peer interaction and social opportunities these programs provide are priceless for motivation. If your local schools do not have such a program, it's vital to search for a way your child can join a social outlet for their music in their teen years.

There may be community groups your child can join or opportunities in your teacher's studio, or you may want to start a quartet or chamber music group with your child and a few peers. In my experience, teens who do not get plugged into this type of experience do not keep playing through their high school years. It's almost a one-to-one correlation. Just like young students need fun and creativity to keep them engaged and motivated, social outlets for music are equally important in the teen years. Helping connect your child to these groups is a great way to continue to support their music development and set them up for success.

Creating the Practice Routine

It's important to create a daily routine around our music practice. This topic always makes me think of my children and brushing their teeth when they were young. Who knows why they resisted doing this so much, but we had some big power struggles over brushing teeth before I learned the following strategy.

To make brushing teeth more palatable or tolerable, we found toothbrushes with cartoon characters that they loved. We found toothpaste with fun pictures on it and with a taste they liked better. We listened to the Raffi song about brushing teeth in the bathroom each night. Eventually, it became a habit to brush their teeth multiple times a day. We needed these extra strategies to make it more tolerable at first, though. We also had a solid commitment that we were going to keep at it until the habit stuck.

In much the same way, children often need creative ways to do their repetitions in music practice. This practice strategy will eventually turn into a habit. They will one day see how careful repetitions help get the results they want.

There are many ways to help young students track their repetitions:

- Bead counters, either homemade or purchased
- Reward charts with stickers
- Moving little plastic animals, coins, or other small items across the music stand or table for each repetition
- Movement after every couple repetitions, such as jumping jacks or somersaults, or go walk somewhere else in the house and back

You may be able to come up with even more. While this may seem inefficient from a time perspective, this helps extend young students' tolerance and ability to focus from two to three repetitions to as many as twenty within a short amount of time.

These short activities away from the instrument, coupled with fun or movement, create a wonderful system of giving little brain breaks to our children so they can come back and focus again. Plus, it makes the practice more enjoyable. I can't state the importance of this enough.

The way each child enjoys counting may vary and will likely change over time, but having some way to mark the number of repetitions works wonders. Some people get quite creative with it.

One parent told me she does a push-up for each repetition her child does. Another said their child delights in putting bows and clips in her mom's hair, so she gets to add a new one for each repetition. She had a hilarious picture of herself with a head full of bows—so fun!

Some practice partners use art as part of the practice sessions. One parent shared they draw one part of a picture for their child after each repetition. For example, if the final picture is a person between repetitions, the parent adds the head, then the body, then the arms one at a time, etc., so that by the end of practice, there is a completed picture.

Stickers can be a much-loved incentive as well. Online and through office stores, you can find reward charts to fill in with stickers as another option. At first, your child may get a sticker for each repetition, and over time you can likely stretch it out to a sticker every two repetitions and eventually every five.

I like to test things out once in a while and see if we can get in one more repetition before needing a counting and brain break.

Are Rewards and Incentives Bad?

I know there is concern over using rewards and incentives for practice sometimes. Much has been written about too many rewards and how that can get in the way of true internal motivation. I ultimately want my students to be motivated by the music itself or their love of playing the instrument.

Here's the reality, though: While a few students may be internally motivated from the start—like the student I talked about a moment ago—for many, when everything is new and hard about the instrument, it can get in the way of them feeling motivated by the music or instrument itself.

When asked at what point they went from feeling like everything about practice was hard to feeling like they could really play, the teenagers we interviewed in Oregon said it was at an intermediate level. At the intermediate to advanced level, I believe students have learned how to practice more effectively and can see the results of their work more easily. In addition, they have enough skills on their instrument that they are becoming more internally motivated by the music they are playing itself.

Until then, having short-term rewards and incentives like stickers help us have an immediate feeling that we have accomplished something—a feeling many students may not feel they have from the instrument itself for quite a while.

A Note to Parents Who Are Musicians

A word of caution for musician parents: Since we know the power of repetition and can often see our child is on the edge of a big breakthrough, it is very easy to push too hard. Please err on the side of too few repetitions and gauge your child's ability to focus as well as their level of frustration.

If your child can really handle a couple more repetitions, great. But please observe closely and make sure that is actually true. I have heard stories of children of musicians who refuse to practice with musician parents or have learned not to trust them when they say, "One more time."

A breakdown in trust can contribute to a lack of enthusiasm, or even resistance to working together in the practice room. This goes back to our definition of positive practice. If we lose the sense of mutual respect and trust with one another, our practice relationship breaks down.

More on Trust in the Practice Room

Dr. Karin S. Hendricks, researcher, award-winning music educator, and professor of music education at Boston University, has done extensive research and writing on trust, especially in music settings. Her book *Compassionate Music Teaching* has an excellent chapter all about how to foster, repair, and think about trust in the music classroom.

It's so important to think about this topic, which is why I reached out to her to ask how she thinks that trust comes into play in the home practice relationship. She says:

> Trust is everything in a relationship—including a home practice relationship. People (children included) need to feel safe to take risks and that includes emotional safety.
>
> It is critical for parents to know *how* to encourage students to go beyond what students imagine is possible, so that they can maintain a trusting relationship.
>
> If they push to the point of pain or fear, then trust can be lost. The "nudge" of a parent or teacher should be about expanding their awareness of possibility.
>
> In a home practice relationship (just as in a music classroom with a teacher), the parent and child are co-learners. They are each learning different things, but they are both learning. So they both need to feel a sense of trust in the other.

This is such a valuable way to think about trust in the practice room and the value we want to place on it. Sometimes, missteps happen and the relationship or trust is damaged. This can absolutely be repaired, but we often need to admit where things have gone wrong and sincerely apologize.

I suggest if you've fallen into negative patterns and are pushing too hard, apologize to your child and spend some time giving only positive feedback during practice and let your teacher do the pushing. After some time, most parents find they can go back to more active coaching once the practice relationship is repaired. Others find they can best support their child by staying in a cheerleading role and letting the teaching role stay with the teacher in the lesson. You can also flip things around and allow your child to teach *you* what they're learning during a practice session.

Of course, we want our children to be successful, improve, and play to the best of their ability. We have to be careful that it's not at the cost of our relationship and ability to work together, though. Trust in the practice relationship is so important, and I encourage you to hold that up as the highest priority.

Where to Start

How do we know where to start with all these ideas? The best way to tell what will interest your child is to simply start trying out ideas to see what works. You may come up with your own uniquely creative idea along the way. That's part of the fun. It's okay for it to be silly. Use what works to keep your child engaged in practice and willing to engage in it again tomorrow.

An important note: Sometimes these strategies work for a short time and then need to be changed up for novelty or because your child's interests have changed. It's good to have a few strategies in mind, or come back to this section if you need some fresh ideas.

I suggest observing what motivates your child in other areas. Is it movement, or is it stickers, or is it games? This observation will help you know where to start. I can tell you that once parents figure out what helps with repetitions in practice, they also figure out a great way to motivate their child to do other things.

One parent in my studio experimented with a simple strategy of adding stickers to a blank three-by-five card for practice and came back the next week, sharing that it worked for all sorts of tasks around the house. Not only that, but it was taking the arguments and cajoling out of the equation and helping the child look forward to earning stickers. "Practice with my child is making me a better parent!" she shared.

Your child will eventually learn the power of repetition in practice. Until then, we can help with ways to make it fun, or at least more palatable.

Being Consistent

When I asked the one hundred practice partners in my research study what the number one thing was that made practice work in their family, the overwhelming answer was being consistent and having a routine.[2]

At one of my workshops, a dad shared with us that their teacher offered a studio-wide one hundred days of practice challenge. At first, they agreed to participate but thought it sounded like an impossible goal. By the end of the one hundred days, though, he said they wanted to keep on with it indefinitely. They realized how much less resistance there was to practice (by everyone in the family) once it became a given that practice *would* happen each day.

A word of caution, for some practice partners, and students alike: The idea of a continual practice streak and counting days like this can backfire. I know for me they don't work well, as I tend to skip a day on purpose (although unconsciously) to take the pressure off. This is where knowing what works for us on an individual level is important. If your child is motivated by one hundred days in a row, great! If your whole studio or class is doing one together, that might help some students enjoy tracking days more than doing this kind of project individually.

The key here is consistency, though, so you don't have to follow this example if it has the opposite effect. Make it work for you. Maybe, like me, you do better to pair up your practice with something else in the day, like breakfast, or have a scheduled time you stick to but without tracking days in a row. Find what works for you and be as consistent as possible—that's the main message here.

Once it becomes an unnegotiable part of our day to practice, we no longer have to waste mental energy deciding if we *will* practice, and we also have space in our day to make it happen.

There may still be days when no one has the energy or patience for practice or when it's hard to get started. However, it does become so much easier when it's just an accepted part of the day. We can sometimes feel that we're "being nice" to give our children a day off of practice. But it's been my experience, and that of practice partners I speak to, that the more we do this, the harder it is to practice the next day. I imagine the thinking goes a bit like this: "Maybe we can skip today too—let me see!" It's key to make daily, regular practice the rule. There will be days when we have to cut things short, or we're traveling and might need to listen to our music or get creative in other ways. We want a rule of daily practice, and then we can take the unusual exceptions as they come. We want it to feel like a strange day when we're not getting in our practice.

Like any discipline—exercise, writing, learning a new language, and many others—the more we do the work regularly, the more it becomes part of who we are and the less resistance we feel to starting.

Remember, not only is this important or a nice suggestion, but the majority of practice partners in my research said consistency was *the thing* that made practice at home with their child work.

Schedule Practice Time

When we sign up our children for a sport, the practice schedule is usually set for us by the coach. In music, our child may have a lesson once a week and maybe a group class or orchestra other days, but our child, with your help, is in charge of setting up practice sessions on their own.

I have learned over time not to take for granted that everyone thinks about this on their own or remembers to do it. Please make sure you not only set aside time once a week to attend your private lesson, but that you also set a daily time for your child to practice for the next class. Each week in the lesson, the teacher shows you the next steps needed to make progress. Then it's up to the student, with family support at young ages, to do those things all week long and make them easier.

You may need a different time for practice each day of the week, depending on your family schedule. You may need to sit down before each week begins to map out when each day will work to practice over the coming week. Post it somewhere so everyone can see, and then it's easier to put it into the family schedule each day. In a perfect world, I would love everyone to have two options for practice time a day. That way, if something comes up during the first one, we still have a second chance. While this may not be possible every day or for every family, it's worth thinking about.

We need time to practice daily to build that routine and consistent practice we just read about a moment ago. This is an important step! Waiting for an open time to appear in our schedule so we can fit practice in doesn't work if we want to be consistent. It has to be built into our day.

Understand What Works for Your Child

There are many, many practice strategies. You will read about a number of them in this book. You will hear teachers and experts recommend many things. After raising two daughters and teaching for twenty years, I can tell you that not every tip or strategy works for every child. I find that creativity is needed with each new student I teach to find just what works for them.

We can approach this with curiosity and notice what works and what doesn't. If someone swears by a strategy and it's a total disaster at your house, that doesn't mean anything is wrong with you or your child. Maybe it will work when your child is older. Maybe it never will. That is not a failure. It's just information that gets us closer to what *does* work. We can cross that strategy off the list of possibilities and move on.

I do encourage you to give new ideas a try. I remember thinking that some ideas would never work for my child and then being very pleasantly surprised. There is a difference between doing what we know helps our child and being close-minded about creative solutions. Talk to teachers, talk to other parents, listen to interviews, and read books about practice. We can all learn from one another's ideas and hopefully unlock what our child needs for success.

With some trial and error and close observation of what works, we can find strategies that help support our child's musical development. The wonderful side effect of all this is getting to know our children and how they learn. We now have strategies to help our children in their schoolwork and other parts of life. It also allows our children to learn how to work with themselves when they're old enough to practice independently. It's a huge gift to them to learn how they're motivated, how they can work through feelings of frustration, and how they can break big problems into small, manageable chunks.

The Details of Setting Up Home Practice

Next are five tips I typically share with new families in my studio. Things I think everyone needs to know as they get started with music lessons and practice together. I hold very loosely to what I expect to be accomplished by young children on their instrument during the first six to nine months of lessons. Instead, I emphasize setting up the environment and the routine. If you can work with your child peacefully and productively and you have made daily practice and listening to music part of your family routine, I have no doubt your child will learn to play their instrument in time. Keeping these strategies in mind and working with good teachers will help us meet our goals over time.

1. Practice daily.

In my experience, at least five days a week is needed for steady progress. While it may take a little time to create a routine around practice and make that a reality, that's the goal I would work toward. Depending on your child's age and attention span, it might even work better to do two short practice sessions during the day.

Do what you can with the time you have. No guilt, please! Even five minutes of practice is better than skipping a day altogether. It's this consistent work that makes progress possible. There is no magic wand to wave that lets us learn a complicated instrument without practice.

2. Let your child help make decisions.

The goal is that eventually your child will practice on their own. How far off in the future this is depends on their age, organizational skills, how self-motivated they are, and your teacher's process for this transition to happen.

However many months and years we practice together, we want to have our children engage their own brains in the process. The point of practicing together is about more than developing skills on the instrument and helping your child follow through on the teacher's assignments. It's about developing the thinking skills to conduct an independent practice one day. If practice to your child is "an adult tells me what to do," this can be a harder transition.

Giving children a choice between the two next things to do, having them draw the names of activities out of a bowl, having them tell you *in their words* what they remember about how to practice a certain assignment, or how they think their piece sounds are all really important to developing practice skills.

We want students to have ownership over their practice. Ownership and independent practice, though, is a long-term goal. We can baby-step toward it with how we treat practice sessions now. Sometimes, practice goes slower if we do things this way. It may take more time to practice on a given day, but in the end, you're helping your child develop as an independent practicer down the road, and it will be worth it.

3. Set realistic goals at each practice.

If you don't have a plan or purpose in mind for a practice session, it can easily drag on without direction. Before you start a practice session each day, know what you want to accomplish. "We are going to check everything off our practice list today" or "We are going to improve something about the bow hold today" or "We are going to work on practicing together with a good attitude today." All of these are valid.

Depending on the day, when we practice, and everyone's energy level, the goals we have may change from practice to practice. I definitely recommend one goal at a time. In my training as a Suzuki teacher, this was really emphasized, as it is so effective.

Identifying and focusing on a goal helps prevent wasted time and frustration. Playing through something aimlessly isn't practice, I would argue. We aren't going to improve something that way.

Your teacher might help you define a goal for the week or even assign one to you. If you haven't been given a specific goal or focus point for your assignments, it's always a good idea to work on one of the following: technique, tone production, rhythm, or expressive playing. Especially with young children, pick one at a time to focus on.

The main thing I want you to take away is how important it is to focus on *something* when you practice to see results. If it's unclear to you what you should focus on, it's likely unclear to your child as well.

4. Check with your teacher before jumping ahead to what's next.

Sometimes practice is going great, and you wish there was something more to work on. It may even seem obvious what to work on next. It's always exciting to learn a new piece or the next part of the piece we are on, and I understand that.

Sometimes, it's truly not a big deal, or a teacher may want a student to work ahead in a sight-reading assignment, for example.

Other times, I want to carefully walk a student through something new to save them, and all of us, time and frustration.

Communication with your teacher is key. If you're not sure if you should wait for the next lesson or move ahead, be sure to ask. It's also a good idea to ask what you should work on if you have extra time to practice.

5. Focus on quality repetitions.

Young musicians are building skills. Many of the skills that are learned at the beginning stages need to be in place (and will still be used) in advanced levels of playing. It's also important to note that often we can understand what we are practicing before our muscles can do it automatically.

For example, for many of us, when we learned to drive a car, it takes all one's concentration just to operate the vehicle and keep it on a straight path on the road. I remember being forbidden from turning the radio knob because I couldn't manage it while driving safely. It would make me swerve to the side of the road and throw off my driving.

Eventually, we learn to drive so well that parts of it become automatic, and we rarely think about them anymore. But at first, it takes all we have just to keep going.

It's very much the same for your child learning to play their instrument. It takes everything they have to keep going at first. However, with time and practice, much of it will become automatic. Then the student can focus on new details. This is the importance of repetition. This is why we spent so much time talking about tolerating multiple repetitions earlier in the book.

Careful, quality repetitions can take some creativity on your part. This will give us proficiency at an instrument that is quite difficult to play. If we can play many pieces with ease, we have the foundation for newer, more complicated things that we will learn in the future.

Conclusion

If you're just setting out to start practice with your child, I hope this chapter has given you some steps for starting off with good habits in mind. It's far easier to start off carefully and set up good habits than to fix bad habits later. We always need to adjust and make changes to our approach as our child's development and technical skills grow, but habits that work with that growth and lead to long-term progress and motivation are key.

ACTION STEPS

- Ask yourself: What do I want my child to gain long term by studying music?
- Think about what new strategy you can use to make repetitions more enjoyable and to build in brain breaks.
- Do you have a practice schedule? How can you make it more consistent?
- What can you use from this chapter to make a difference in practice this week?

CHAPTER SEVEN

A New Way to Look at the Practice Relationship

I AM WRITING THIS BOOK A YEAR INTO THE COVID-19 PANDEMIC. This past year has been an intense one for parents working with their children. Many of us have been working, parenting, and even schooling all in the same space with each other day in, day out.

We likely have been juggling many roles at the same time, from home. We might feel tired. We might feel shorter on patience. We might need some extra support and inspiration for ourselves as we strive to give that to children we are practicing with.

We might have felt these things before the pandemic; maybe we'll have circumstances in the future that will feel this way too. I hope this time has taught us all a little more about how to keep music in our lives through challenging times.

As teachers, we have been showing up on screens of all sizes in people's homes to give lessons. We may have seen a glimpse, for the first time, of what practice looks like at home versus what we see when families come to our studios.

Before we get into specific practice strategies, it's important to look at how we, the adults practicing with our music student, think about practice and our role in it. That's exactly what we're going to dive into next.

I love how Brittany Gardner writes about this in her book *This Will Help You Grow: Advice & Encouragement for Suzuki Parents*: "As a parent, I had to practice my relationship with my child as much as (or even more than!) we practiced the specific assignments given to us by the teacher."[1] As we think about practicing that relationship, here are three perspectives that can help set us up for a healthy working relationship between practice coach and student.

The Three Practice Perspectives

There are three important perspectives, or mindsets, that we can adopt as practice partners to make our practice sessions more positive and productive: connection, a belief that our child can learn and improve, and a focus on teamwork. I believe they can really transform practice. If you're new to practice, then you can use them to start off in a productive way. They will help you establish positive interactions in the practice room that support learning, progress, and the relationship you have with your child.

Many teachers and practice partners figure out how to navigate these perspectives by trial and error. You may have discovered a couple of them yourself already. It's my goal to save the frustration and guesswork for you if I can, and maybe shed some light on why some of these strategies work.

It's key to focus on these three points: connection, a belief that our child can learn and improve, and teamwork.

We can start by asking ourselves the following questions:

- Do we see practice as a way to connect with our child?
- Are we trying to find out how they learn, focus, and stay motivated?
- Do we encourage effort and see mistakes as a way to learn?

- Do we take time to celebrate how far we've come, even if our child still has much to learn?
- Do we see ourselves as being on the same team, working together with our child to accomplish the assignments for the following week's lesson?
- Are we involving our child in the process of practice, or giving directives to complete without asking them to take on any decision-making roles?

I encourage you to reflect on these questions and any others that come up for you as you read the rest of this chapter. Think about how they apply to your practice sessions right now. Think about how you might develop them in yourself as you work with your child in music practice. Keep in mind, as Brittany Gardner wrote, that we are practicing the working relationship with one another as much as, or even more than, the assignments on the instrument at times.

How Do We Start if We Want to Make a Change?

To adopt these new perspectives as a practice coach, I recommend being very intentional in how we think about practice sessions. Sometimes, as a parent, I need to consider new research about the brain and child development and what that means for the behavior I am seeing in the practice room. I have to challenge my beliefs about how children learn, or should be treated, so I can best support them and create a positive learning environment.

Here are a few things I didn't yet know when I was first practicing music with my own children:

- The importance of built-in brain breaks.[2]
- Children learn to regulate emotions through relationships. If I stay calm and help them name emotions and feel them, it helps my child get back to a calm state.[3]

- Outbursts and meltdowns are often a sign of overwhelm or stress.[4] I can help reduce stressors in practice, whatever those might be for my child.
- The part of our brain that helps us organize and plan practice often fully develops in our early twenties. My child will likely need extra support with tasks like this.
- The energy I bring to the practice room has a big impact on my child in the practice session.

Because there's so much new research about the brain, and how children learn since we were children, some of the old models and ways of thinking about focused work for children have changed. I think my own generation was taught to think of many problems that we experienced as students to be flaws in our character. Science is showing us this is just not true. Many adults my own age went undiagnosed until adulthood with some of the following:

- ADHD
- Sensory processing disorder
- Autism
- Dyslexia
- Anxiety disorders
- Dysgraphia

We cannot expect children to simply "try harder" and be able to overcome learning challenges. Tools, strategies, and sometimes professional support are needed. Access to correct diagnoses or resources can be a real challenge for many families, and we should all advocate for them in our communities. In the meantime, we can at the very least realize a child can be trying their very best and not be able to do what we're asking without additional support.

It's hard to let go of these patterns and assumptions we grew up with. This is deep, personal work. My hope is that as you read and learn more, you might be able to reevaluate some of the messages you were raised with about how children learn and develop that may be outdated now that we know more about child development and the brain.

I'm not here to tell you how to parent. I'm here to share with you what helps students learn and what I find, and research shows, helps parents and their children work together successfully in the practice room.

When applying all this new information, keep in mind that we don't have to be perfect parents. In fact, there is really no such thing. The authors of the book *Raising a Secure Child: How Circle of Security Parenting Can Help You Nurture Your Child's Attachment, Emotional Resilience, and Freedom to Explore* tackle this issue head on:

> Time and again in our work with parents from all cultures, of all ages, in every demographic group, we've found that exposing these false beliefs (of perfection) and the parenting practices they encourage helps people relax into raising their children . . . when you can relax into bonding with your child, you radiate a calm, responsive confidence in your parenting that builds your child's trust that you are there for her and teaches her that she'll find others who can be trusted in the same way for the rest of her life.[5]

My goal and message to you as a practice coach and parent is for us all to shift our primary focus from results to helping our children feel supported and successful during their practice sessions.

I hope we also grow to enjoy the process along the way. We must let go of any pressure to be the perfect practice partner and relax into our role of helping our child learn instead.

As we talk about the practice relationship, I want to be clear I'm not talking about focusing on all of this instead of focusing on practicing the instrument. We are doing both, at the same time. I want to emphasize them, though, because I don't think it's possible to just focus on the instrument in practice without coming up against the health of the practice relationship at the same time.

ACTION STEPS

- Reflect on how you are already including connection, a belief that your child can learn and improve, and teamwork into practice sessions.

- Read upcoming chapters to find ideas to implement in your practice sessions.

- Take in new information about how children learn and develop and use it to help make practices both effective and supportive of our relationship in the practice room.

CHAPTER EIGHT

Focus on Connection

When we talk about what we can do as adults to make music practice productive, this quote from Fred Rogers sums up what I'm aiming for: "There's a world of difference between insisting on someone's doing something and establishing an atmosphere in which that person can grow into wanting to do it."

I'm often asked questions about how to help children develop motivation and focus, or how to get to the next level or move on to a harder piece of music.

For very young children, the discipline and hard work of learning an instrument may be a real challenge. These are often skills we learn over time, through our practice sessions. There are exceptions, but very young children often need someone to help them learn to do this well.

The goal is to help cultivate a love of music along the way while we learn to practice effectively. It's to help create an atmosphere that is positive, engaged, and connected so children eventually do feel motivated on their own.

There are many pieces to this process that we can support as the practice partner. They include making time in the schedule to practice, coming to the practice ready to focus, knowing *what* to practice, knowing *how* to practice, and celebrating our successes along the way. We can help these skills and abilities develop by being there with our children as they hone their practice skills.

Students will need reminders of what they were asked to do in their lesson. They may need someone to take the assignment list from their teacher and prompt them or remind them what to work on next. Students will likely also need an adult to help them notice when they're getting frustrated or stuck and might need a brain break or a movement break.

Practicing an instrument is hard work. It takes complex planning and thinking skills. It's frustrating and sometimes overwhelming to students who haven't yet developed their practice skills. All of this can be true, but we can also love playing the instrument at the same time.

This is where the importance of connection comes in. As a child, feeling connected to an adult who is helping us figure out how to practice is important. Knowing we have someone who is there with us so we don't have to go through our big emotions or our frustrations alone is key.

Being present and available whenever possible during practice is a huge help. Our children are learning to work with themselves. They might need reminders of what comes next. They may need some coaching or prompting about how to break down their practice tasks into smaller, more manageable chunks. They often benefit from feeling someone is seeking to understand the struggles or frustrations that might be coming up for them in practice.

Part of what we're doing as the practice coach is helping spark the desire for learning. The teacher has mapped out how to get to the next step in the student's musical journey, and we're helping coach our children through each step involved.

The teacher can't do the actual day-to-day work for us, though. Often, students need help to make the assigned steps easy to take action on, or to remember all the details involved.

This can feel like a big responsibility. Some students need more guidance and help than others. This is not a failing on anyone's part; they will thrive with more help and hands-on connection with a caregiver during practice.

It's easy to see practice time each day as an intense moment of getting things done and checking off boxes on a to-do list. It can be a challenge to get our child to focus and work hard. But really, there's no way to make our child do any of that; instead, we're trying to set up an environment in which learning can happen. Eventually the desire to learn and improve comes from them.

What I learned the hard way is the importance of treating practice with our children as a chance for connection rather than a battle of wills with one another.

For many of us, practice might be a rare moment of concentrated one-on-one time. That can be a real gift. But it's a gift that's easy to miss if we forget to focus on connection.

Let me state it more simply: Be there with your child. Help them structure their practice. Remind them of what they need to do. Give them space to make some decisions and make some mistakes, but be there when they need you. Coach them through the big emotions that come up so they can get back to a place of calm and focus. Doing this together is a powerful way to make practice more positive and productive.

This connection in practice only happens if we're intentional about it. We have to choose each day to make it a priority to connect through music. We can focus on the quality time together, on learning about our child, and on deepening our relationship with our child. This doesn't mean we don't care about progress on the instrument or set that aside. It means we do both; in the same way we can connect and read, we can connect and practice.

Here are some ways to think about cultivating connection to your practice at your house:

- Start practice with a connection point. Read a story related to music together. Listen to music together and talk about what you liked.
- Play a quick game that involves cooperation.
- Give high fives, hugs, and thumbs-up—acknowledge your child's effort.
- Point out the progress you see, or simply reaffirm that you believe your child will make progress with time and effort.
- Articulate the fact that you enjoy spending time together in practice.

When I interviewed cello teacher Brittany Gardner for my *Beyond the Music Lesson* podcast a few years ago, she shared something that echoed my own experience practicing with my dad. Neither of us remembered specific practice tasks we did with our parent, but we did remember what it felt like to spend time together with our dads in the practice room.

I don't personally remember any details of working on new pieces, challenging rhythmic patterns, or playing better in tune, but I'm sure we did all of that. I do remember the time we spent together. I remember my dad staying calm when I was losing my patience and getting frustrated. I remember the persistent belief my dad had that I would in fact learn if I kept working at it and paid attention to the details. I remember him challenging me to hold myself to a higher standard as I got older and more advanced. This certainly provided a wonderful model of what a great practice parent does. This is the power of focusing on connection and the lifelong impact it can have.

I truly believe we all come from a place of wanting the best for our children. I believe we all want them to succeed. I think sometimes it's easy to let the immediate goal on the instrument get in the way of connection in the moment or thinking about how it feels to be on the other side of the practice room from us.

Permission to Be Human

In music practice, some tasks may feel harder than others. Some days will be more difficult, and some will feel easy. There will be areas where you feel more equipped to help your child, and others will take some research and thought. Some days your child will show up in the practice room tired, or hungry, or out of sorts.

Some days *you* will.

We are all allowed to be human. Not every practice is going to be wonderful. Showing up consistently and connecting is key.

It's important to make the commitment to being there with our child through the ups and downs of practice as they learn and grow. If nothing else, we want to be there to say, "I'm here. We'll figure this out together."

With younger students, you may be very involved in every detail of practice. For older students, you may just need to be a presence nearby. Some students need a body double, which is a term discussed often as a way to help students with ADHD, but I think it's helpful for all music students. Parent coach and advocate Elaine Taylor-Klaus describes it this way: "Sometimes we don't need to say or do *anything* in order to be helpful! Often, all our kids need to get the job done is another body present. That person can be working alongside on a shared task, or doing something completely separate—it just depends on the circumstances."[1]

For some of us, this is what our children need to be successful in practice once we no longer need to remind them of the technical tasks to work on. Others need someone to prompt them about what to do next so they don't get stuck transitioning from one segment of practice to another.

We get to help our children learn how to practice. We're also teaching them that we're there for them. That even if we don't know the answer, we can find someone who does. You don't have to be a musician to support your child's practice. Showing up to support them and to work together is all they really want.

ACTION STEPS

- ♪ Find ways in each practice session to connect with your child.
- ♪ Being present is key. Your child may simply need reminders of what to work on and to have someone there to support them through doing the work of practice.
- ♪ Remember, practice time can be a chance for quality time. "I'm here with you" is a powerful message.

CHAPTER NINE

A Belief That Our Child Can Learn and Improve

MOST YOUNG MUSIC STUDENTS DON'T START OUT KNOWING HOW TO practice. It's a skill they will learn and improve at over time, just like so many other skills in life. Marilee Sprenger, author of *Social Emotional Learning and the Brain*, puts it like this: "If you go to the gym and work out, your muscles get stronger. The same is true of your brain: the more you work at learning and problem solving, the easier those things become."[1] Believing in the potential of the child in front of us in the music room to learn and improve, no matter what they can actually do at this moment, is key for helping support their continued growth.

Growth mindset is a term coined by researcher Dr. Carol Dweck that is likely familiar to many parents and educators.[2] Embracing this mindset and believing that we, and the children in our lives, have the ability to learn, grow, and change is so important. We see growth in music learning all the time. We can remember when it was hard to simply hold the instrument. We remember when we couldn't get a good sound no matter how hard we tried. We think about pieces that used to feel daunting and difficult, that now feel simple and easy.

Sometimes, though, it's harder to think about how we put this idea into action. How do we cultivate a growth mindset in a very tangible way in our practice sessions and in our home? We may know it's something we want our children to develop, but have we considered that we, the practice coach, may benefit from focusing on it as well?

I want to be very clear that what we're talking about here is not blaming our mindset if things need improvement. We're not treating mindset as a magic wand that will fix everything. What we *are* talking about is holding strongly to our belief that with time, effort, and good teachers, we believe improvement is possible.

Let's consider four different ways to put this idea into action in the music room and in our family environment.

1. Praise the effort, even more than the product, that you see in practice.

If we believe improvement happens through the effort we put forth, and we believe it will help us improve, then praising effort over results is key. Are we working on the assignments from our teacher? Are we working consistently? Do we see our child putting forth effort, even if there's some frustration involved? If so, we can trust the process and know we'll get there eventually. Growth will come.

In music practice, we are focused on quality practice and on building skills that will be a foundation for many more advanced skills to come. Building these skills, with attention to detail and setting up good habits, takes time and effort. Outward signs of growth may take time and happen in very small increments at first. Such tiny measures of improvement might be unnoticeable from day to day but can add up dramatically over time. If we trust the process, put in the daily effort, and follow our teacher's guidance, that improvement will absolutely come.

2. Let your child see you learning and growing in some area of your life.

Cultivating a belief that with time and effort we can improve and grow can become a project for the whole family. What are the adults in the family working on? Perhaps training for a race, fixing something around the house, learning a new skill, such as a new language or instrument, or reading and learning about a new topic for work. You may have another project in mind. The key is for our children to see other family members working to learn a skill and all the ups and downs that come with it. This is a powerful example to set.

I always think about Angela Duckworth's wonderful research on grit and how she applied it to her own family when thinking about this topic. As Duckworth learned more about how grit is developed and its impact, she created in her family something called the "hard things rule."[3] Everyone, even adults, had to have one thing they were working on that required diligent practice and hard work. In this way, the family environment was one in which everyone could share in the experience and the ups and downs of doing something challenging.

3. Notice how far you've come so you can see the growth.

It's easy when we see only tiny increments of growth each day to forget how they add up over time. Sometimes I will recommend students in my studio and their family to watch a recital video from a year ago, or look at their lesson notes and what we were working on many months in the past. This is often very illuminating. Just like it's hard to see how tall children are getting when we see them every day, it's hard to see progress when we're part of the daily tiny steps moving forward. It can be so encouraging to look back and see the progress in a tangible way.

Tiny increments of progress add up to big results over time. In his book, *Atomic Habits*, James Clear emphasizes the huge outcomes we end up with if we simply try to improve 1 percent each day. He writes: "It is so easy to overestimate the importance of one defining moment and underestimate the value of making small improvements on a daily basis. Too often, we convince ourselves that massive success requires massive action."[4]

Remember the analogy of planting a seed that we discussed in Chapter Six? We know the seed we've planted is in the ground and we know that we are doing what we can to help it grow. At the very least, we are learning better how to help it grow every day. Long before we see a sprout poke out from the dirt, we will continue to water, weed, and make sure there is enough sunlight and we'll trust the seed will grow in time. This analogy can help us remember that first the growth happens under the surface. Roots are shooting out and growing underground before we see the visible growth. But we know how plants work, so we trust the process.

This is the same thing we're doing as parents and practice partners. We're providing the ingredients and we're planting the seeds and nurturing them with what they need. And then we trust the process that some of the seed will sprout and grow.

It's no different in practice.

I've taught for two decades and can trust that if families follow what I assign and put in the work, they will see results and their child will learn. We'll see what we want to do to modify our strategies and make them work for each individual student, but I have no doubt they will learn and improve. I know as a parent it's harder to trust the process.

I hope I can share some of my assurance with you that it *will* happen. Stories from other parents and families who have been there can help too. Practice may look imperfect along the way, and we often need reassurance that we're still moving in the right direction.

4. Realize that mistakes are a way to learn.

Another way to put growth mindset to work is to think of mistakes as a way to learn. Many of us tend to think of mistakes as something we have to be ashamed of or to avoid. This is true both in practice and other areas of our life. Sometimes, we learn the most from things that we struggle with or do imperfectly.

If we feel like we're destined to repeat our mistakes forever no matter how hard we try, it's tempting to give up. This is true for learning an instrument, a new language, a difficult math concept, and so many other things. However, if we see the mistakes as part of the learning process and commit to continued work using our mistakes to teach us, this helps us stay committed long enough to see progress happen.

It's absolutely key to developing as musicians to be able to tolerate mistakes and see them as a way to learn. In Daniel Coyle's *The Little Book of Talent*, he writes: ". . . being willing to risk the emotional pain of making mistakes is absolutely essential, because reaching, failing and reaching again is the way your brain grows and forms new connections."[5] Avoiding mistakes at all costs comes at a price of stunting our growth.

Sometimes our children have perfectionist tendencies and get extra discouraged by their mistakes. If we're honest, some adults fit that description too. I personally have to remind myself that mistakes are a powerful way to learn. They're an important part of our learning process. It helps me to keep my eye out for stories about musicians and athletes, and any others I can find, who share their process. Noticing how high achievers first struggled or wished things were easier is a powerful reminder. Let your child see you make mistakes and treat yourself with grace. I know this is easier said than done.

We can start to see these principles in action all around us. If we see our efforts pay off, and that our mistakes are helping us figure things out, that is so powerful. It gives us a great way to embrace the process of learning.

Students can mistakenly feel like everyone around them has an easy time with everything and they are the exception to that rule. We know that couldn't be further from the truth. However, the best way for our children to learn that is to see it in action.

I often hear about this challenge with children of musicians. They see all the adults in their lives playing their music with ease. The student has no way to know, or truly understand, that their parent was also a beginner once. It can seem like being able to play well is something you either have or don't have. Students can feel like something is wrong if they don't immediately play at a professional level. The perspective that it took years and likely thousands of hours of imperfect playing and hard work to get there isn't clear to them.

It's important to share that we had to make mistakes and learn through the same kind of practice too. Making sure students have groups of other children in the learning process to make music with and to observe helps as well. We can find opportunities to share imperfect playing of our own, or practice process when learning something new to give perspective. Sharing in many ways that everyone starts in the same spot and without knowing how to play can be very reassuring to young students.

Focusing on the learning process as a family and working on developing it together can provide great motivation on the instrument. If children see our effort pays off, and that our mistakes are leading us to figure things out, it sets a valuable example. It's a great way to see learning in action and embrace the process.

ACTION STEPS

- Have everyone in the family pick something to work on and share the process together.
- Talk often in the practice room about how our mistakes teach us and help us learn.
- Focus on praising the effort you see in practice rather than just the results.
- Truly hold on to the belief that with time, effort, and following the teacher's guidance, your child can and will learn.

CHAPTER TEN

Focus on Teamwork

No one sets out to argue with their child at every practice or signs up for an activity that's going to purposefully cause a daily battle of wills. However, it's very easy to fall into this habit and for practice to turn into a daily, scheduled argument with our child. No one is enjoying the process when this happens. What I encourage families to focus on is developing a sense of teamwork in practice.

I suggest thinking about practice like this: You and your child are on the same team, working to accomplish a goal for the next week's lesson.

Our role as practice coach will help assist when things are challenging and help the children we are working with succeed. Let's talk about how to make that happen.

First, spend time observing how your child learns and what motivates them. Here are some questions to consider and reflect on:

- Does your child prefer to practice what is easy and comfortable, or what is new and unfamiliar? (Hint: I see students on each side of this who strongly prefer one or the other.)

- Does your child get caught up in mistakes and not want to keep playing, or do they race through and seem not to notice the mistakes at all?

- Does your child learn best when they can see what they are learning demonstrated for them? When they hear the music right before trying it?
- Does your child crave positive feedback? Does it work best to give silent, nonverbal feedback?
- What kind of reminders help them? What kind shuts them down?

There is so much to learn about how our child can practice best. Some of it is based on their age and stage of development. Some of it based on how they will learn best for the rest of their life. What I found as a parent is that learning how my children learned, through music practice, carried over into school subjects and into many life skills. It gave me so much information on how to work with them outside of the practice room, and that was such a gift. It saved us hours of struggle in other areas of life. More importantly, we learned to work together to solve problems as they arose, and my children learned to rely on me as a support person for challenges in their lives.

I think the best outcome from all of this was my children learning to work with their own strengths. Over time, through ongoing practice and working with your teacher, some areas of struggle will get strengthened and will improve. I believe working with our strengths is always a good place to start.

Effective Teammates in Action

When we are on a team, we want to balance out each teammate's strengths and weaknesses to accomplish the task at hand. We want to assess what skills each person has and focus on those strengths.

Perhaps your child is enthusiastic and loves playing through what they have already learned, but maybe they tend to be resistant to new assignments. Focusing on review is a good thing, as they'll build up a strong foundation of skills with this review and reinforcement of what is going well. As a practice partner, we know we also need to get our new assignments going so we can keep improving. When we see this happening, we can help support that area of practice and make it more palatable for our child. We can bring in games or incentives and make it fun or easier for them. We might help them break down new assignments into bite-size chunks.

The opposite is also true. Perhaps our child loves a new challenge and diligently works on their new assignments but is resistant to things that are already learned. As adults, we can understand the excitement for the new; however, we have the long-term perspective that we must build the foundation underneath to support all the exciting things still to be learned.

Just like a swimmer doesn't learn a new stroke and then stop practicing those they already know, we are building on our skills as we go. This is also true of how we learn to speak as young children; we still use the same words for the rest of our lives, even while adding more complicated words to our vocabulary. In music, we often need to continue to work on technical skills even after we learn them. Adults can help the review and polishing of technical skills feel more tolerable with games, incentives, and tracking systems until the student understands the value of this review process on their own.

The repetition does take deep focus. Also, we want it to be done with careful thought, not rushed through while our brain is busy thinking about other things. This is a big task. Frustration sometimes happens for students who feel like they're being asked to so something they don't understand or don't have enough information to follow through on. They may not be able to put that into words, so it's important to notice frustration and give multiple ways to think about the same assignment.

It's also frustrating not to be given independence when you *do* know what to do. I hear this a lot from families I work with. Of course, one of the challenges is that sometimes students feel they know all there is to know before that is actually the case. This is when it's important to work with your teacher. What would they expect the child to do independently at their current level? I suggest starting there.

There is a continuum for working on a practice team together with the child doing most or all of the work on one end, and the practice partner heavily involved in all tasks on the other. As we learn to practice together, we learn to adjust the levels and may be on different sides of that continuum depending on the task

ADULT-LEAD ⟶ CHILD-LEAD

Adults helping with music practice can help support the areas that are hard so they can be developed over time. This may only be needed for certain parts of practice. Your child may need support to stay on task or to organize a plan for accomplishing all their assignments.

Your child may need support getting started or remembering the details of the practice assignment. Observation first can really help with this. Teammates, on a healthy, functioning team, support each other and appreciate each other's strengths. It's also important that our child will not practice with us forever. Eventually, when our assistance isn't needed, we will gradually hand over ownership of all practice details to our child.

I recommend doing this bit by bit. Work with your teacher to be sure your child is ready for a certain task to be done independently.

Going from one end of the continuum to the other in one swift move is often not as effective as gradually allowing for more independence when your child is ready. Depending on your teacher's philosophy, your child may be assigned independent practice from the start, but that doesn't mean they won't still need this kind of support at home.

A final thought about teamwork: I suggest thinking of yourself as a practice mentor or coach rather than the practice judge or jury. If we spend practice time handing down rulings, such as "Nope!" or "Wrong!" and other comments like these, we may be right, but it really only causes frustration. Instead, point out what to work on next, show them what is going well, and help support them through the process.

If you really need to do something with the mistakes or areas you're noticing, and some people really do, I suggest writing down what you notice. As a teacher, I notice them all too, but I have had training and years of practice to pick what to prioritize and how to prevent overwhelm. You can absolutely work on this as well. Notice what your child's teacher wants them to focus on. Write down the rest. One thing at a time will help us effectively move forward. It's important to remember that handing down rulings and pointing out all the things wrong is going to cause friction and get in the way of working as a team.

Practice Is Its Own Skill

There are many skills involved when learning an instrument, and our teachers will help us learn and refine them over time. But how do we learn them? Yes, we have to practice individual skills. We also really need to practice *practicing*. We need to learn *how* to practice.

Sometimes, I hear parents ask the experts how to overcome various practice challenges with their children and have heard answers like, "Well, you just make them do it." I guess that may work for some people, and good for them. But if it were that simple, there wouldn't be books, parent discussion forums, and constant conversations about how to actually make that happen.

I remember trying some of the strategies I learned in my own teacher training courses when practicing with my daughters, and my frustration at the fact that we couldn't make them work for us. As a teacher, I was sure something was wrong with us, but it turns out my child didn't fit into neat boxes about how practice works. I tried to force her and thought she was misbehaving at first. I really learned over time, though, that's not how she needs to practice. We will talk more about how you can work with the unique needs of your child later in this book. All of this was a hard-learned lesson for me, but it sure taught me as a teacher that sayings like Just Do It make nice slogans for shoe companies, but don't work for everyone when it comes to practice.

As we think for a moment about what skills we are developing, here is a short, incomplete list to ponder about what students are learning in music lessons:

Instrument Skills

- how to hold or sit at the instrument
- beat and rhythm
- music theory
- tone production
- fine motor control
- large motor movements
- audiation and hearing the kind of sound we want to produce

Practice Skills

- time management (when will you practice?)
- organizational skills (how will you practice everything assigned to you?)
- focus (can you actually use the time you have productively and well?)
- discipline
- problem-solving skills
- delayed gratification (it may take many practices or many weeks to learn something well)
- critical thinking
- perseverance or grit

I often start teaching music to preschoolers. I am quite confident they will develop those music skills with my help in lessons. However, I really need the family's and parent's help to develop the practice skills at home throughout the week. There may be many years until some of these skills are solid and dependable. Even for those who catch on more easily, it tends to take a while. This is why I'm going to enlist the help of parents, like many of you, to guide practice and help your child learn how to do these skills.

Remember, research tells us that many executive functioning skills live in the prefrontal cortex of the brain and are not fully developed until our early twenties. This is why our role is so important, even if we're not musicians.

What we do want to think of is that learning to practice is its own skill. It's a skill of equal importance to learning the technique of our instrument. Together, they support the ability development of an excellent musician.

Through focus on teamwork, a belief that growth is possible, and connection with our child, we can keep progress moving forward while maintaining a healthy, supportive environment for practice.

ACTION STEPS

- Think about your perspective as a practice partner: Are you fostering connection, teamwork, and a belief that improvement is possible?
- What is a first step you can take to put these ideas into action?
- When you see challenges come up, try to separate learning to practice from learning the instrument. Both are important, but they need different kinds of practice.

SECTION TWO

The Five Stages of Practice and How to Use Them to Our Advantage

CHAPTER ELEVEN

The Phases of Practice

Over the two decades I've taught the violin, I've had many conversations with parents and students about practice. How to set up good practice habits. What to do if something about practice is a challenge. How to make progress and enjoy the process.

After so many years, and so many conversations, patterns start to emerge. When a family asks for help because they are overwhelmed with practice, I find myself asking them a series of similar questions to see how I might help.

Practice, as we've already established, is a discipline. It's its own skill. A skill I have found is helpful to think about in smaller parts. We plan for practice, we transition into practice, we do the work on our instrument, and we bring practice to a close. And then, from time to time, we reflect and make sure we're getting the results we want from all this planning, coming and going, and hard work.

When we understand how each part of practice affects the other and learn to use them to our advantage, it can help our practice go more smoothly. It also teaches our children how to eventually use these parts of practice for themselves and their own goals in the practice room.

Our goal is to develop practice skills and instrument skills and have our sessions be as productive and positive as possible. That's no simple task. But we can work toward this goal together.

What you'll find in this section of the book is my process for helping families set themselves up for great practice habits, and alternately to help get our practice on the right track if needed. It's the process I use with families in my studio, and it's been developed in the lab of my studio, with my own children and many families around the country who have put these ideas to work for them.

If you find it helpful, you can also refer to my workbook that gives colorful visuals and space to write and reflect called *Positive Practice: 5 Steps to Helping Your Child Develop a Love of Music*. It can be an effective way to think through, and reflect on, how each of the phases of practice we'll talk about here apply to your children.

As we dig into more details about the phases of practice, I want to first acknowledge you as the practice partner for the amount of thought and work this takes. It's the job of the music student to practice. However, in our supporting role, we can have a profound impact on the environment they practice in, how they understand what makes a productive practice session, and in helping develop practice skills.

When we are practicing with preschoolers, we are doing most, if not all, of the work of planning practice sessions and guiding our child through each one. As students get older, they will gradually take on more and more of the responsibility for practice.

Your teacher will assign work to be done at home during the week, which becomes the road map for what to practice until the next lesson. Then the follow-up happens at home as our child puts in the time, with our support, practicing throughout the week.

In my experience as a teacher, it's very rare that a student just automatically understands how to do all of this or takes to it easily without support. Some students will, and that's great. Others won't have much success without a supportive adult or mentor to help. In either case, it's to a student's advantage to have support as they learn to make the most of their practice time. If you're in a supporting role like this, this section should help clarify how to help support your child's practice routine from start to finish.

Over the next few chapters, we'll discuss the five phases of practice. I'll also give you action steps to think about for each one that will help you take steps to support your child as you work together to improve or structure practice.

I've heard from many teachers who have been taking new groups of students through the workbook based on this framework so their students and families are set up to understand how to practice from the start. Many parents have shared that they really love these ideas and find the concepts help demystify what we're talking about when we refer to "practice."

One mother, a parent of a piano student, shared that she and her husband thought they were being really great parents when they would insist their child sit at the piano and keep going as long as possible. Eventually, her son would cry, and they'd let him up off the piano bench and try it again the next day. That became their practice process inadvertently.

You may recognize that routine from your own house, or maybe from practice of your own when you were growing up. I think it's very common from the number of stories I've heard like this.

If we're not intentional about it, for some people, the phases of practice can look at bit like this:

A parent or child, maybe even both, feels apprehensive about the upcoming practice. We know it's time to start and we know we need to remind our child to get started, or it may not happen. We cross our fingers that it goes well. Sometimes, the student knows it's almost time to practice but wants to keep reading or riding their bike or getting more done on another project they're working on. In other words, they want to stretch out the time they have before starting practice.

We may start out with this worried state and then need to negotiate with one another to actually get ourselves into the practice room to get started. Maybe it's ourselves as a musician we're wrestling with. We know we want to have practiced, but there are many other things on our mind.

Hopefully, once we finally get into the practice room, we have some time of making music and getting our assignments worked on, and then eventually we wave the white flag and surrender. We decide we'll try again tomorrow.

I hear stories about scenarios like this often in the work I do. It's easy to fall into habits and patterns like this without meaning to, or to be unsure how to turn things around.

We can find ways to make practice less of a chore and get a more motivating cycle of practice going instead. Ideally, we want to create a feeling of momentum, and hopefully even moments of enjoyment and fun, as part of this process.

As you read about the phases of music practice, I hope you have some of your own aha moments. I hope you can think about each of the specific parts of a practice session and help your child by engineering a practice routine that works well for them and their needs. Let's look at each part of the practice cycle in-depth together.

CHAPTER TWELVE

Planning Changes Everything

When we go to a dance rehearsal or a soccer practice, the coach has a plan of action for the practice or rehearsal time. There are certain skills that will be worked on, there will be routines or plays to practice, and there will be time to cool down and debrief at the end.

The longer I teach, the more important I think it is to talk about planning our practice sessions too. What will we warm up with, what drills or exercises we will cover, and what pieces we will work on improving.

In fact, my top two tips for success in practice long term are to be consistent and to take a few minutes to plan your practice sessions in advance. Pianist and educator Stephanie Bramble Chevalier says that focusing on this idea was particularly transformative for her teaching and for studio parents as well. When asked how she wants parents to think on having a practice plan, she said: "It's not enough to have a number one point—it must be accompanied by a plan. Quite simply, what is our goal today? What are we trying to accomplish?"

Most professional musicians I've talked to or heard interviewed have some plan of action before they start their own practice. The approach varies, and some pros will have a detailed plan on paper or in a spreadsheet, while others have a routine that has become habit and is more of a mental planning process that they remind themselves of as they get started.

A great resource to think about this in-depth is *The Mindful Musician* by Vanessa Cornett. In it, she shares her ideas about practice and performance and also shares some planning templates. If you have a teen musician in your home, this is a great resource to connect them to.

Students who are practicing more independently can also ask their teacher to help them make a plan for practice, or they can make a plan together with their parents and put it into action on their own.

Young students who lack experience in planning practice will likely need more help. Just like we wouldn't send a young soccer team out onto the field to lead their own practice and expect disciplined and organized results, young students will likely need help organizing and planning no matter how independent they are about working on the musical skills assigned by their teacher.

Of course, not every young musician has someone to help them plan their practice and follow it. In this case, as teachers, we may include extra help with this in our lessons and want to talk about it with extra care while we're teaching.

What I've found is that with a few minutes of planning and strategizing, we can help our children and students make practice sessions more effective, more organized, and more productive.

Without a plan, we may tend to waste time, to stare blankly at our music stand, frozen by too many decisions, or to feel unsure where to start. It can feel a bit like driving or walking somewhere and being unclear of the directions. We may wander the right way eventually, but we may also cause ourselves extra time and frustration in the process if we don't have a clear path forward.

It's tempting to think this step isn't really necessary. We'll just practice at home like we did with our teacher in the lesson, right? Except without our teacher there guiding us through to what's next, many students and families can feel stuck. They may notice they're not seeing the same results at home. Or it's hard to follow through and implement the assignment that seemed easy in the lesson. Spending just a couple minutes on this step can help change the effectiveness of our practice in a profound way.

How to Start Planning Practice

If you're a parent, or practice partner, I suggest starting with a goal for yourself. How we show up in the practice room can have a big impact on the tone of practice with our children. Remember back to our perspectives of connection, growth mindset, and teamwork. This is a great place to start to be intentional about how we incorporate those ideas into home practice.

You can fill in one of the following blanks as you think about the goals you have for yourself as you help with practice:

1. Today I will be:
2. Today I will focus on:
3. Today I will set the tone of:

Some examples could include focusing on being patient, totally present, or putting away phones and devices or turning them on airplane mode while we practice. We could work on the kind of comments or feedback we give during practice. Everyone likely has something they can work on to bring their best selves into the practice room to work with their child each day.

Set Practice Goals for the Day

Next, we'll move on to goals for our child. It helps keep practice sessions focused when we give ourselves goals to work toward. Often, there's a goal that our teacher helps us set for the week, which makes it easy to choose and know where to start.

Some parents will write this somewhere in the practice space each week and point at it when their child needs a reminder. It can also serve to remind us, in the helping role as well, so *our* efforts remain focused on the goal at hand.

There are many possibilities of what to focus on. Some include posture, hand shape, playing in a relaxed way, getting a beautiful tone, how we're holding our instrument, and more. If you aren't sure what to focus on, please ask your teacher. I know I'm always happy to clarify this question for families; after all, it's my goal for their music practice that week to move things forward in a productive way and help them improve their skills.

Some prompts I suggest for planning practice goals for the student are:

1. In today's practice, our main goal is:
2. Three things we should try to accomplish today:
3. Something we didn't get to yesterday and shouldn't forget about today:

You can answer these prompts before you get started on practice each day. Alternately, you can fill them out at the end of practice each day, for the next day's session. That's my favorite way to do it. Then the practice we just finished is fresh in our minds and we can make a plan to carry it forward to tomorrow.

If your child is around ten to twelve years old, this may be an activity you can do together. This way, your child can see the process and eventually feel empowered to do this on their own. Helping them see the process, gradually letting them have input, and eventually taking on the role of planning practice themselves is our ultimate goal.

Structuring Practice: An Introduction

As we think about setting our practice goals, I also want to take a moment to talk about how we structure our practice.

There are a few different ways to do this, but I want to suggest three simple models in this chapter. The bullet point list, the pie chart, and time chunking.

I'm going to explain each one in a progression from a beginning student to a more advanced student and how I typically see them change over time. However, you may find it valuable to use any of them, at any age, and at any level. Just like everything else in this book, I encourage you to make this your own, do some experimenting, and focus on what works for your child and your family.

The Bullet Point List

1. ______________________
2. ______________________
3. ______________________

The first model for how to structure practice is a simple bullet point list. When students are starting lessons, they usually are given a short list of skills to practice each day. In my studio, with new violinists, that often looks like rhythm assignments, how to stand in playing position or rest position, and sometimes the beginning steps of holding the bow and violin separately. Your list may look different.

You teacher may have a written list to give you about what to practice. Or they may ask you to take notes during the lesson. Then it's up to you to come up with your own list based on what happened in the lesson that day and any further instructions given by your teacher.

Taking a couple of minutes to turn your notes from the lesson into a bullet point list of what to practice can be a great way to make sure you get to everything your teacher has assigned you during the week.

I've heard some parents share that they take these notes and put them into a spreadsheet or digital document. Then each week going forward, they simply update the document with the new assignments from the teacher. This gives them a template to work from.

A handwritten list works great too. The key is to take written or verbal notes from your teacher and turn it into a list of practice tasks that's easy to follow in the practice room. This list will take the guesswork about what to practice out of the equation.

It lets you get right to work when it's time to practice. This system usually works well for quite a while, maybe even the first couple years of lessons.

Eventually, it may feel confusing to try to get all the tasks you're assigned into a simple list like this. There starts to be many different assignments, and it may feel unclear how to get to them all. You may spend the same amount of practice time each day that you used to, or even more, but not feel that you're getting to everything. That's when we're ready to think about the pie chart method of structuring practice.

The Pie Chart

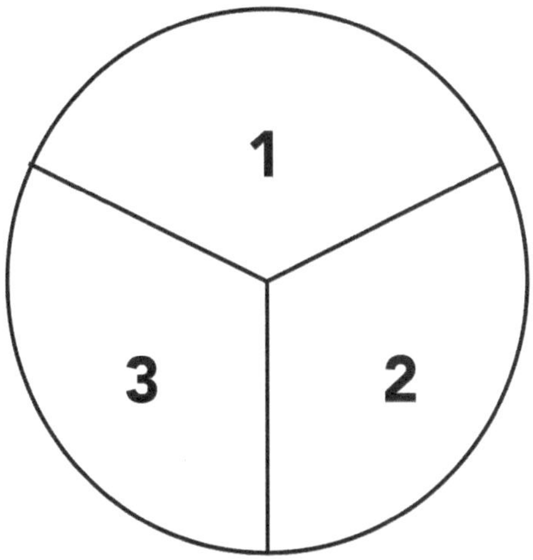

1. Scales, Note-reading, Exercises
2. Renew
3. New/Polishing

Another way to divide up our practice tasks for planning purposes is the pie chart method. Moving from a simple list of practice tasks to dividing our time into a few groups of assignments usually becomes necessary when there are a few categories of assignments like multiple scales, note-reading pieces, maybe orchestra music, and a number of pieces to be worked on at various levels of mastery.

If we make a bullet point list at this stage in our lessons, it might look very long and feel overwhelming to get to everything. We might get through the first part of the list but not make it through everything most days. We may work on a certain portion of the list each week, while others get ignored, often simply because there isn't enough time.

The solution is often to divide our practice time into three or four chunks of a pie chart, as you can see in this graphic at the beginning of this section.

To make things simple to discuss, we'll assume that a student is assigned to practice for thirty minutes. Our three segments of the pie chart will represent one-third of practice each, or ten minutes each in this case.

Section one is where you'll put scales, note reading, and other technical exercises assigned by your teacher. At least to start, you can plan to spend about one-third of your practice time on these. You may want to set a timer for ten minutes and when it goes off, it's time to wrap up what you're doing and move on to the next segment of practice.

My advice to my own students is: If you finish these assignments in eight or nine minutes, it's probably okay to move on early and give some additional time to other areas. If you finish these assignments in three or four minutes, it probably means more time should be spent on them. Of course, some of this depends on what your teacher is assigning, so you can adjust as needed, depending on their recommendation.

Segment two is where I put refining and polishing assignments. If you maintain a list of pieces to play in orchestra, a group class, or a rotating review list, this is where those assignments can go. A focus point or goal of the week for this section is a great way to help deepen skills and make things easier. Working with your teacher, you can find a way to rotate through this material so it gets learned and worked on each week but doesn't take your whole practice, thus leaving no time for other assignments.

Segment three is reserved for new pieces of music. Some of my own students would spend their whole practice on this if there was no planned structure to practice. Others feel more comfortable working on things they know well and would avoid it completely. Having a piece of our practice pie chart dedicated to new music helps us balance all of this out. It prevents it from taking over, and it prevents it from being avoided. It's great for students either way.

Check with your teacher for details about what should fall in each section if you're not sure. This is a guideline, not a hard rule. The percentages will likely change when we have a recital coming up or an audition for orchestra or other special situations to prepare for.

The key thing, though, is to find a way to group assignments and think about how to get as much done as possible. This strategy keeps us from finding a long list of assignments daunting, and it helps us effectively get through all our material.

Thinking about how each assignment you were given falls into the segments of our pie chart, making a plan and setting a timer for ten minutes at a time or fifteen or whatever you choose can help us see when it's time to move onto a new activity and come back to the assignment tomorrow. Over time, you will start to see what is realistic and maybe when you need to think about increasing your practice time as well.

An additional note: The pie chart concept is giving us a method to fit in all our assignments in an organized way. It's also important to make time to play something we love just for fun. Leave time for exploration and improvisation on your instrument. If your teacher doesn't give you specific assignments along these lines, saving a few minutes at the end for creative exploration and musicmaking is a great idea. Many students enjoy this as a way to cap off a practice session after their assigned tasks are done.

Eventually, our practice assignments don't fit in three categories neatly either, and that's when we move on to the next strategy called *time chunking*.

Time Chunking

As a student's list of assignments grow, bullet point lists and pie charts may not be as helpful anymore for planning practice. When this happens, I suggest moving to a time-chunking approach instead. Here's why I think it helps:

Dorothy DeLay was a world-famous pedagogue who taught violin at the Juilliard School of Music and has famously taught such performers and educators as Itzhak Perlman, Sarah Chang, Paul Kantor, and Brian Lewis. I came across a list of her recommended practice routine for students in a fascinating book about her teaching, *Teaching Genius: Dorothy DeLay and the Making of a Musician*, which specifies by the hour what to practice:

> The first hour is spent on basics—articulation, shifting, and vibrato exercises for the left hand and various bow strokes for the right; the second hour is for passages from repertoire, arpeggios and scales; the third for etudes or Paganini; the fourth on a concerto; the fifth is for practicing Bach or the student's recital repertoire.[1]

There were short rest periods built in as well as a recommendation to leave out specific hours on days when a student had orchestra practice.

We're talking about young nonprofessionals for the purposes of this book, so I am not recommending in any way the same length of practice times for your child as for those musicians who studied with Dorothy DeLay. Maybe someday that will be appropriate, but that's up to your teacher to tell you and gets worked up to slowly over time to prevent injury and to build stamina. What I do think we can take away from this is the idea of thinking of practice in organized chunks of time.

In Dorothy DeLay's list, we don't see a random assortment of practice tasks spread out over many hours. We don't see an arbitrary time assigned to practice without a breakdown of what to do. The practice is focused, and similar activities are grouped together. We can, and often should, do the same thing in our own practice when the pie chart approach doesn't serve us well anymore.

I like to think about putting this to scale and making each hour of her plan into a ten-to-fifteen-minute chunk of practice for students who are starting to practice anywhere between fifty to seventy-five minutes.

Time-chunking practice may look like this:

10 minutes
10 minutes
10 minutes
10 minutes
10–20 minutes

For simplicity's sake, this time we are basing our chunks of time on a fifty-to-sixty-minute practice. Again, this is based on your specific teacher's recommendations and not a strategy for beginners. Please start with the bullet point list and pie chart for younger students.

When your child does get to this point, I recommend mapping out their assignments in these time chunks. I often do this with my students in lessons, and if you ask your teacher, they can likely help you to do this as well. For my students, it might look like:

- scales
- note reading and rhythmic training
- sight reading and orchestra music
- polishing pieces and new music

This is very individual, but I think it's helpful to see one example of how it might break down.

Setting a timer and moving on to the next part of the practice once the practice chunks have been mapped out carefully helps students organize their time. It also ensures they're not rushing through assignments.

Time chunking can work well for students during busy times too because they can divide up their practice chunks during the day at various times, rather than all in one long session, and still practice very effectively.

For example, if it's hard to find a whole hour open at once in their schedule, they may be able to get in multiple short sessions between homework assignments or divided up before and after school. This strategy helps us avoid the all-or-nothing thinking that if we don't have a full forty to sixty minutes or more to practice, there isn't any point. Even one of these blocks of practice is better than skipping a day altogether.

By the time this type of practice strategy is used, often students are becoming more independent practicers. They may still need your help, though, to plan out their practice, and you might be able to assist by talking them through the process of grouping assignments and assigning time chunks to them.

Students may also find it helpful to make a practice plan for the week and come show you so they can get some help or coaching with the executive functioning portion of the practice process that we have already talked about in the first section of this book.

Planning our practice is the best way I know to use our time effectively and accomplish our practice goals. In my experience, this takes some of the mystery out of practice and to get our assignments done for our next lesson. Taking a few minutes to plan our goals for each day's practice helps us stay focused. Thinking about how to get to everything on our list helps us be productive.

ACTION STEPS

- Do you currently have a process for planning music practice? Does your child?
- Think about when you will plan practice and how much support your child may need to do so effectively.
- Which type of planning would work for getting to all your child's practice assignments: the bullet point list, the pie chart, or the time-chunking technique?

CHAPTER THIRTEEN

Getting Practice Started

IF YOU'RE LOOKING TO IMPROVE PRACTICE BUT AREN'T SURE WHERE to begin, I suggest we start by looking at the way we get practice started. This can be a powerful way to set the tone and make a big difference in our whole practice session, especially with young children.

Being very intentional about how we begin, and later end, practice can go a long way toward helping you build a strong habit of daily music practice with less conflict.

How the Brain and Emotions Are Involved

The start to practice often sets the tone for our whole day's work with our child on the instrument. If I start out my practice in an argument with someone, that's likely not going to put me in a state of mind to think deeply, to focus, or to take in new information. In fact, research shows us it may not be possible for our child to access the logical, thinking part of their brain when emotions are too high.

The Whole-Brain Child is a great resource to learn more about this. The authors write that "when a child is upset, logic often won't work until we have responded to the right brain's emotional needs."[1] Even if we feel like talking about emotions is too touchy-feely, and we just want to get to the work of practice, this research suggests that it's through addressing emotions that we can actually get to the productive work in front of us.

In their book, Dr. Daniel Seigel and Dr. Tina Payne Bryson recommend helping name and acknowledge the feelings your child may be having and then moving into the logical discussions about what we need to do after that. Sometimes we have to give our child the space and time to get back to a calm state before they can get to work on their instrumental assignments.

Remember back to our negative practice cycle? We want to avoid having a feeling of dread when it's time to start practice or feeling like practice is a scheduled, daily argument. Instead, we want students to have access to the logical thinking part of their brain so we can make progress in the practice room.

It's important to note that it's not your fault, as the parent or practice coach, if practice starts out less than ideally. But you, as the adult, can likely change the way practice starts and set up a positive situation for practice in the future. You have the experience, wisdom, and resources to find and implement a better way. If we're not sure how to make practice more positive, our child surely doesn't either.

Transitions

One challenge that comes into play at the start of a practice session is that many young children can have trouble transitioning from one activity to the next. It could also be a challenge for us as the practice partner. This can be especially true in young children. Specific learning differences can make it more difficult for some people to end one activity and move on to a new one than others. Individuals with a diagnosis of ADHD, autism, anxiety, or sensory processing disorders can especially have a hard time with transitions, although difficulty with transitions alone does not necessarily mean one of these diagnoses is present.[2]

What seems like your child not wanting to start their practice might in fact be difficulty with these transition moments. A parent recently shared with me that their child happily goes into the practice room when it's time to practice, but it takes ten to fifteen minutes for that same child to really be ready to focus on their instrument. Maybe a child comes right in the practice room but is then too wiggly to start, acts silly, or seems to be stalling getting to the actual work we're there for.

This story was a good reminder to me that we don't just see difficulty with transitions when students struggle to stop other activities and come into the practice room. Sometimes, our children take a while to get into the flow or mental state to get their assignments done. The deep thinking and deep work that are required to practice well just isn't ready to happen yet. We may need a way to transition into our practice successfully.

Create a Transition Ritual for Practice

When these transitions are a challenge, it's often wise to ease into practice with a starting ritual. For example, when I sit down to write, it can take a while from the moment I sit at the computer until words start to flow and I can be productive.

There are a few things I do to speed up that process. I have a plan for what I'm going to write about, and I know exactly what my starting point will be. I tend to jot it down for myself at the end of a session so it's there for me when I get started the next day. Then it feels like I'm continuing on from the previous day in a very natural way.

We can do this for our music practice as well. Coming into the practice room with a list of things to practice and no clear way to start can feel overwhelming. I think some of the procrastination related to starting practice comes from this reality.

Our transition ritual, along with the planning we did from the last chapter, will give us a plan of action and help us get into productive practice much more often. It gives us a bookmark in a way. We are not starting from nothing each day; instead, we've hit pause the day before and then can find our place and keep going today.

The other thing that's part of my transition ritual for writing is putting on a playlist of music. It doesn't matter what it is, but once I hear the music that has become part of my starting routine, it gets me in the frame of mind to write. I still need transition time for the words to start to flow, but I waste far less time this way.

In a similar way, we want to set up a ritual or routine that helps your child get into the productive part of practice. We want to find something that sends a signal to our brain and body that it's time to begin.

Here are some ideas for transition activities:

- Listen to the current piece your child is learning as they set up their instrument and materials.
- Listen to music and keep the beat or dance to the music.
- Draw a picture while listening of what the music makes you think of or the story it tells.
- Practice tapping out rhythms by clapping or using rhythm instruments.
- Work on pre-note-reading activities assigned by your teacher.

- Read a book about music together or a short chapter of a book about a composer or famous musician.
- Write out practice tasks for the day on a white board and talk through them.
- Pick a practice game together to incorporate into today's practice.
- Start out with one simple activity on the instrument that stays consistent from day to day even as other activities change.

This list can help you get started, and you can also observe how your teacher helps your child transition into their lesson for further ideas. The key is to choose something that is enjoyable and helps everyone get into the frame of mind for focusing on practice.

Every child is so unique. I still have to be creative to see what will work for every student I teach. Don't worry if it takes a little trial and error to find what works best.

In addition, don't be surprised if an idea works for a little while and then you need to change things up a bit. With new developmental stages and interests, your transition activity may need to change from time to time. You can come back to this list for inspiration anytime.

For many students, establishing a predictable routine will help them ease into practice. A transition ritual can often cut down on conflict and frustration for everyone if getting started has been a challenge.

Learning to ease ourselves into focused, disciplined tasks is a skill that everyone can benefit from developing. For some students, and practice partners, it just happens, but for others, we need to be more intentional. This skill will especially come in handy when our child is doing their own independent practice one day and will need to get themselves started in the practice room.

Give a Warning

If I'm deep in thought, reading a book, or working on a project and I know I need to practice, I have to give myself a little time to wrap up what I'm doing before I can start. I might need to remind myself that in ten minutes I need to be ready to get the instrument out and begin.

If you could see my thought process, it would go something like: "If I don't start practice soon, I'm not going to get to it today. I'd better wrap this up and start soon."

Then I'll putter around and save my document, finish reading my chapter, or make a note to myself about whatever I was thinking about so I can come back to it later. I may need to tidy up any mess I've made. I may need to use the restroom or get some water. Often, I will make some coffee before I start my own practice if I'm honest. All of this is giving me time to leave the old task behind and also gear myself up to get to work. I love having practiced, but the starting is not always so joyful.

If you are the practice partner at home, you may find you need to do something similar before you practice with your child. It takes some mental fortitude some, if not all, days! You may relate to this when you think about starting exercise, your own work projects, household chores, or any other focused activity you do.

Here's the reality: Your child really needs the chance to do this too.

So often we've mentally prepared ourselves to practice with our children but then say, "It's time to practice!" To them, it feels out of the blue. "What? Now?" we might hear.

I've read this from sleep experts for children as well. As adults, it seems very logical that every night there is bedtime, and yet when we say "It's time for bed!" it's met with much protest. "What? Again? This is the worst news I've heard all day!"

Practice is no different. In both of these cases, what helps the most is to have a ritual that signals to the child bedtime, or practice, is coming. It eases the abrupt change and instead helps our child mentally prepare for what's coming next.

We talked about transitions already and what some potential transition activities are. I think it's important to add that a time warning can be really helpful too.

A ten-minute warning, especially with a timer that will go off and signal practice time is here, is the best tip I can give you. This way, we don't have to announce it like some kind of town crier who only brings bad news. We can let the sound of the timer deliver the instructions that it's time to start and make things more pleasant for all of us.

There's something so much less personal about a timer beeping versus a parent saying it's time to practice. So, if your child has a strong reaction to a verbal reminder, this is a great strategy to try. Often, students will respond better if we tell them they have five or ten minutes until we start and then set the timer. The timer can then deliver the news when time is up.

This strategy gives our child the same room to wrap up, tidy up, and change gears that we likely give ourselves as adults. If we need it, children likely do too.

It's important to acknowledge that we don't always "feel" like practicing at any moment, and I think it's important to allow for those feelings. I suggest you share how you can relate too. Maybe there are things in your life that you know you want to do, and feel better after doing, but find it hard to get started on.

Talking about these feelings helps us acknowledge and move through them. I always want my students to know it's perfectly okay not to want to start—there's nothing wrong with feeling that way. We're still going to do it, but allowing for emotions in the process is really important for helping them get to that state of calm and starting to practice.

A Getting Started Challenge

The best way I've seen to help my own students and their families who are experiencing conflict around getting started in practice is to have a "getting started challenge." Usually, this is something I assign in the lesson when I hear getting started has become a point of conflict.

I give the student a little chart with the days of the week. Each day that they come to the practice and get started, they put a sticker there. It's important to say that we're not rewarding being happy when we start, but rather being willing to come in and get started with our transition activity. All feelings are allowed.

As adults, we can make the structure of the practice work for our children and keep it positive, but it's up to them to come willingly into the practice space to start. I encourage a fun reward for getting five or more stickers on the chart. Something that would fit in your family's value system.

In my studio, some ideas have been baking a favorite treat with a family member or going on a special trip to the library and picking out a fun book. Other families have let the student pick out the family movie for the weekend. It doesn't have to be expensive or complicated. Families reported that their child was not fighting getting started anymore after about a week or two of putting positive attention toward cooperation at the start of practice.

ACTION STEPS

- ♪ Reflect on how you get practice started in your house. Are transitions into practice difficult for your child?
- ♪ What kind of transition ritual or activity could you add into practice to make the start of practice a bit smoother?
- ♪ Think about your own mental process before you do an activity that takes discipline and focus. How do you mentally and physically prepare?
- ♪ What insight does that give you as you think about helping your child prepare to get started in the practice room?

CHAPTER FOURTEEN

The Daily Work of Practice

WE HAVE DISCUSSED OUR GOALS FOR THE DAY, WE HAVE OUR strategy for structuring our practice, and we have gotten ourselves started in a way that eases our child into practice or helps us transition effectively.

It's time to get to work and make progress in the practice room.

There are so many books and resources available that address how to practice. In this chapter, I want to focus on how to get work done while we support our child as a whole person and keep our practice relationship strong.

Often, our role as the practice partner is to help our child stay focused or move from task to task effectively and to make the practice assignments manageable to complete at home. Our child has to do the work, but we are there to coach them through *how* to actually get it done.

Our primary goal is often to see that practice actually happens, and then, over time, our goal often shifts to supporting them as they learn to do it on their own.

If our assignment is to repeat a practice task ten times, our child might need a reminder to do that and then might diligently be able to work on it. Or it might take a lot of creativity, encouragement, and persistence to actually get ten repetitions done each day. However easy it is for a student to focus, and regardless of how much support they need at any given moment, my biggest goal for my own children and students is that they develop a love of music and learn to play their instrument to the best of their ability along the way.

I don't want to lose sight of those two goals while accomplishing the tasks in front of us in the practice room. Often, when we're learning a complicated instrument, a lot of the fun and sense of accomplishment from the instrument itself comes *after* we've put in a great deal of work and gained some solid skills. Sometimes we love the process; sometimes we love what we get out of the process.

I always want practice to happen with the whole child in mind. I don't want to insist on getting work done at all costs. Nor do I want to say that we don't need to work hard in the practice room. It's a balance to cultivate the love of music and a habit of working hard. It absolutely can be done, but I'll ask you to keep an eye on holding on to both of these goals.

Changes over Time

If your child is young, I recommend keeping practice short and positive. This is the time to build a routine and create an atmosphere of teamwork, connection, and growth mindset in bite-size chunks. Just like we talked about creating a link between warmth and affection and reading for young children, we want to cultivate warmth and connection in the practice room around the instrument we're learning. When your child is young, you will likely be involved in more aspects of planning and following through on practice and all the day-to-day details.

Alternately, when your child is a teen, I recommend the rules of what to practice and for how long be decided between your child and their teacher. However, there are still ways you can support them in the work-hard/love-music equation.

One way you can do this is to help your teen remember to make time for practice. Don't be surprised if you have to tell your child to practice all through their teen years. My parents had to remind me all through high school to practice, and many of my professional musician colleagues say their parents had to do the same thing.

Often, structuring time and organizing schedules is not easy for students even if they do know how to practice independently once they get started. This is one big way you can help. We've talked many times in this book about the role of executive function skills, and here is a huge area where teachers often need your help.

How You Can Help

In my workbook *Positive Practice,* I ask families to consider which part of the daily work of practice holds their child's attention the most. It's a great way to be helpful during the working phase of practice. While your child is working on their assignments, you can help by noticing when they struggle to focus and what they're doing when they enjoy the process and could keep going for longer.

This takes some careful observation. You may not know what that is as you're reading this today, but practice with our children gives us an opportunity to learn what motivates them and helps them learn best.

Some possibilities are:

- When there is something to prepare for a performance.
- When there is an audience to play for in practice (even pets or stuffed animals).

- When playing with a steady beat (tapping or metronome), a backing track, or piano accompaniment.
- When playing without any of those things.
- When being giving clear, frequent feedback.
- When being allowed to self-analyze.
- When using a timer to help with short, focused bursts of work.
- When no time pressure is added.
- When taking frequent brain breaks or allowing for movement.
- When working for longer without interruption.
- When teaching someone else the skill, like the practice partner.
- When seeing a visual cue or reminder.

I encourage you to notice what works for your child. If you are practicing with more than one child, it will likely be different for each of them. Your child may benefit from practicing in a really different way than you do, if you're a musician.

If we take the time to observe and notice what works, and allow for changes over time, it helps our practice, because we can start to work with the needs of our child instead of against the way they learn and process things. We can allow for the fact that their approach may look different than we expected. We can help them be successful and productive in the practice room.

Sometimes, it's the hardest for parents to do this when we learn really differently from our children. It can sometimes be easier to run a practice session with a child who learns just like us because we can just do what helps *us* learn. For example, if a parent finds games helpful for practice and the child does as well, everyone is happy and understands how to practice together.

It can be a real challenge if your child learns in a totally different way. I remember a parent like this in my studio asking, "Who doesn't like games during practice?" This prompted a lively discussion in one of our parent meetings as parents spoke up about how either they or their child were not a fan of practicing that way. I think it was an eye-opening experience for us all to think outside our perspectives.

With that being said, sometimes it's also challenging if we see many similarities between the way we learn and the way our children learn. We may both get frustrated at the same things when practicing together and then don't have a way to naturally balance out the ups and downs during a practice session sometimes. Or things that frustrate us about ourselves cause us stress when we see our child having the same challenges.

We want to find what works so we have moments when our child says something along the lines of "Wow, that went by really fast today." Then we can figure out how we got there. What were you doing in that practice? How did you approach it? Maybe it was just a random thing that day, but often there's something about the way we worked together that we discover helps them get into what psychologist Mihaly Csikszentmihalyi calls a "state of flow." I think musicians reach a state of flow in practice when they start to lose track of time and get lost in their practice. They become totally engrossed in what they are working on rather than watching the clock or simply counting repetitions.

That's what we want to notice. How do we help our children keep their attention and build their focus? How do we help our children stay engaged and make progress until they are able to be more independent in their practice sessions?

Spending the time to figure out what is motivating to your child, at least at the current age and stage of development, has huge payoffs. If we can figure out what makes us work hard, we have the ability to make more progress on the instrument.

What Helps and What Gets in the Way

Another factor to consider is how your interactions with your child help or get in the way of getting things done. We might use ideas or strategies that are wonderful for others but might get in the way of this particular child focusing or doing their best. Sometimes, we get into patterns of interaction like bickering about details or practicing when one of us is tired or exhausted. We need to rethink our approach. It's often a good idea to take a step back from time to time and take an honest look at this.

Remember that research I conducted with over one hundred practice partners sharing what it was really like to practice with their children? A huge part of the practice struggles in my research were happening in the parent-child dynamics in practice. I suggest we set aside how we think practice *should* go or what we *should* be able to say to our child through our feedback and take the scientific approach.

What actually helps them focus? What actually helps things go smoothly and maintains a healthy working relationship in the practice room? Sometimes it's a very specific kind of feedback, and sometimes it's not giving verbal feedback at all. It really varies. In the workshops I've run for parents and teachers, I hear all different versions of what works for students. Some ask their practice partner for very specific, blunt feedback. Others thrive when their parent only gives positive comments. Still others just need a practice partner in the room cueing them on what is next but can give themselves the constructive feedback needed to practice effectively.

What we want to notice is how our child responds to different types of feedback. I would argue practice is not the time to teach a life lesson about accepting feedback in general, although practice over the years will teach that.

Practice is for working on skills on our instrument. It's the time to see what feedback works, in this moment in time, to make the most progress and stay motivated.

If a certain kind of feedback causes practice to break down or is overwhelming to our child, that is counterproductive. That type of reaction is giving us information that we can use to make practice more productive and positive. We want to work with our child's needs to get the practice tasks done, while supporting them as human beings and developing young musicians.

Sometimes in lessons, I will have a conversation with parents and students together about how to work on particular practice spots. Sometimes, we'll come up with a nonverbal reminder to use in practice together. Sometimes, I'll ask a student to let their practice partner help them through a certain spot that they'd rather do alone but actually need support on. Other times, I'll ask the practice partner to let the student be more independent on a given task and be accountable to me at the next lesson.

If your teacher doesn't address this directly in your lessons, you can have the conversation at home together.

Questions like:

- How can we work on this together, as a team?
- Here is the assignment—what can I do to remind you of it while you're playing?

- What does your teacher want you to improve?
- How did that sound to you?
- Did the specific task we are focusing on improve?
- Is that what you wanted?

These types of questions allow for conversation and emphasize that we're working as a team. We don't want practice to just be "following orders" from adults. That type of approach can eventually cause pushback and rebellion to practice. Not only that, but we want our child's own brain to be engaged in the process as they learn their instrument and learn how to practice.

This approach is not a waste of practice time, even though I know it can feel like it drags things out a bit. Remember our goals of both learning to practice *and* learning the instrument. Let's dig into more specific ways you might give feedback during a practice session.

CHAPTER FIFTEEN

Productive Ways to Give Feedback

When I speak to groups of parents, I often ask them to submit their questions in advance. A very common question I get is, "How do I give my child feedback in practice that they will actually accept?" In my own research, practice partners shared that when they gave feedback—maybe even the same feedback the child got from the teacher in the lesson—their child would shut down or react negatively. One parent shared that if they said anything *positive* to their child about playing, their child would melt down. That certainly doesn't make any logical sense, so what do we do with that as adults who support young musicians?

In Edmund Sprunger's book *Helping Parents Practice*, he gives a great explanation of why feedback can be so challenging for a child to receive, especially from a parent or caregiver who they rely on for feelings of security and love. What I have learned from his work is that I may have a great relationship with my students, but it isn't *me* they rely on for belonging and safety and love. It's their family. So if they disappoint me, that may be too bad, but it doesn't feel the same as the feeling of disappointing a parent.

Even though as parents I don't think any of us want our children to feel that our love for them is tied to how they are playing their instrument, this can be an unconscious worry for students or even come across that way accidentally if we're not careful.

In addition to these important considerations, Sprunger writes, "Children have a deep wish for things to be instant and easy and are frustrated when then aren't. A child's strategies for getting out of the difficulty and struggle of work may include fussing in hopes the parent will back down, ignoring in hopes that she will forget, and other types of unpleasant behavior."[1]

You can see how giving useful feedback to our children in home practice can get very complicated, very quickly. We want to keep these considerations in mind as we find out what kind of feedback works best for our child.

What is the point of giving feedback at home? Let's focus on a term I learned in my early childhood education background called *scaffolding*. It was coined by Jerome Bruner to talk about the way we support a child while they are learning a new skill, and then gradually remove that support when it's no longer needed. In his book, *The Scaffold Effect*, Dr. Harold Koplewicz explains how to use this idea in action, and I think it very nicely sums up how we can think about helping in the practice room and giving feedback: "Parents are the scaffold that provides structure and support for the child as he or she grows up. They are there to protect and guide, but they don't impede learning and risk-taking."[2]

If we're not careful, our approach to helping our child learn in the practice room can absolutely get in the way of our child learning how to take risks and potentially make a mistake as they learn, or it could help so much that they don't need to think for themselves in a way that's appropriate for their age. It's important to be mindful that we're not just pointing out flaws or insisting on compliance when we give feedback. Our real goal is supporting the development of skills and then eventually, when we are no longer in our practice coach role, being assured our child has those skills to carry forward on their own.

Types of Feedback to Consider

You can learn a lot about ways to give feedback in practice by observing your teacher. Please remember, though, that your child may hear those same words from you in a different light and with a different need for acceptance and security, so your approach at home may need to vary a bit. What might come across as rude or overwhelmed behavior from our child might actually be our child communicating their needs to us.

In Doug Lemov's book *Practice Perfect*, he and his coauthors recommend a number of great strategies for giving feedback as teachers that I think can help us, including: nonverbal feedback, "what, not who" language, the next right thing, and positive feedback, among others.[3] Here's how I recommend applying these ideas as a parent or practice partner of a music student when you practice together or support their independent practice skills.

Nonverbal Feedback

Nonverbal feedback can be a powerful tool, and there are a few ways to think about giving it during music practice. Sometimes in lessons, I'll ask a parent and their child to work out a hand signal and agree on it together with me. Then the parent will give the signal to the student during practice instead of needing to audibly interrupt. I think there are two things at play here.

First, it takes an intense amount of concentration to practice. A student is likely thinking about both of their hands, the music itself, how they are standing or sitting, rhythmic counting, and much more. If we could see a thought bubble above their head, it would be filled with many things at once that they are trying to manage and shift their focus between.

If we start talking while all this intense mental work is happening, it can totally throw off that focus. I like to explain it like this: If you are doing long division with pencil and paper, and then someone comes up next to you and starts saying random numbers—"Ten, three, eight, five . . ."—forget it, there is no way to continue. Your child likely feels this way if they react dramatically to being interrupted while playing. Or maybe they simply have to stop and can't continue on.

Your child may need feedback to practice well. It's our role to figure out how to deliver it in a way that can be used. It might be best to practice small chunks of music and then give your nonverbal cue. The power of nonverbal feedback is that your child is more likely to be able to take in the reminder and keep going without getting derailed. Even if we think it shouldn't throw them off, in my experience, universally, it does.

The second thing that often happens with nonverbal feedback is it depersonalizes things a bit. It helps us communicate what we need to do without all the emotional aspects we already discussed.

Here are a few ideas for nonverbal feedback you can use right away in practice. I already mentioned working out an agreed-upon hand signal, which can include pointing to the bow or any other part of the instrument the student is supposed to be watching as they play. You could write a reminder like THUMB on a notecard or sticky note and hold it up. You could make a small sound like the click of a pen each time a repetition is done correctly. You could move one item, like a paper clip or coin, from one bowl or side of the music stand to another for each successful repetition. There are many ideas that work. Giving feedback without vocalizing it can be a very effective strategy. I recommend trying it to see if it helps your child practice.

What, Not Who

Another way to make our feedback more effective and thus help our children make progress is to phrase our feedback in an impersonal way. Rather than "You need to bend your thumb!" we can say "Remind your thumb to bend" or "The thumb is learning to bend—can you remind it?" It feels very different to be on the receiving end of this kind of feedback.

Violist and educator Laura Sinclair has studied this topic in-depth and shared with me in a recent interview that her research and experience has taught her that anytime we use the word *you* in our feedback, it can get in the way of getting the results we want because it feels too personal. "As adults, we have developed the ability to separate the self from criticism," she says. "A child is still learning that ability, and thus needs our help by keeping our feedback as neutral as possible. This allows the child to stay emotionally regulated and focus on the task at hand."

Personal feedback can cause students to feel defensive or feel like they need to argue, likely for all the reasons we discussed about their need to feel secure and loved by the parent they are practicing with. Using "what, not who" language tends to diffuse this. It also more quickly gets to the issue at hand and helps us focus on our practice assignment. We're trying to improve both our instrument and practicing skills. Let's focus on that and take out of the equation any feeling of a personal attack because of the language we use. This makes a huge difference and reduces conflict while letting us get more done with less drama. It also supports our relationship with our practice coach rather than causing it stress. All of this is a win-win and can't be emphasized enough.

The Next Right Thing

It's easy sometimes to see the ten things our child should improve on and point them out after they finish playing something for us. However, it can feel very overwhelming to be on the receiving end of this list of flaws being directed our way.

Part of my training is to see all those things that need improvement, but to pick one of them to address at a time. Especially for children, one thing might be all they can literally handle to focus on. I think this same mentality can help us in the practice room. And I will let you in on a little secret: it was 100 percent harder to do this with my own children than with my students.

Even if it feels challenging to change our approach, it's really worth it. If it helps teachers—whose opinion our child is less sensitive to—to use this strategy, it can make an impact for us as the practice coach.

By talking about the next productive thing to do, we can direct our child to the next step in their practice and remind them of their goal for that assignment beforehand, maybe even nonverbally.

So instead of "You need to fix your posture, your bow was crooked, and the sound wasn't great," and any other negative or "constructive" things that pop in your head while watching or listening, replace it with "Let's play this section again. Please focus on keeping your bow straight while you play."

This is just one example, but you can use this template:

Let's play __________ and focus on ____________.

All the things we saw that were needing work are still true, but we can train ourselves to say the thing that is most helpful instead. It's a process but one worth working on.

If You Just Can't Help Saying It All Out Loud

If you're a musician or very detail minded, and you get antsy when you can't verbally get out all those things you just saw, I suggest writing them down instead. This can be very helpful. All the potential points to talk about aren't taking up space in our head that way, and then we can pick from the list what most lines up with the teacher's assignment for our child that week.

You might try writing and taking notes as your child plays and then simply respond with what you would like them to do next using the formula above. For some reason, I can do this easily in my head with students, but I had to get it out and down on paper with my children. Give it a try!

Just like that concept of scaffolding, we are helping provide structure and support but trying not to get in the way of progress. We want to allow space for our child to make mistakes and learn from them. Keeping that role in mind can help as we choose what to say to our child when it comes time for feedback. Will it help? Can they do that next? Is some of what we're observing going to need to be addressed over time or little by little? Those are important questions for reflection and sometimes for our teacher.

Positive Feedback

Giving positive feedback doesn't mean saying everything is great, even if there are many problems. It certainly doesn't mean false praise, which most students can usually see right through. It does, however, make a huge difference to point out what is going well. I've found with students that simply pointing out something I saw go well, even if it only happened briefly, causes them to want to do it more. That is the power of pointing out the positive.

You can use this idea too by looking for one true thing that you see is going well. It can be small to start: "You were really focusing that time!" or "I can hear an improvement, let's keep going." There is almost always something positive we can say. Maybe our child made it to the end of the piece and didn't get lost. Maybe their posture or hand position improved. Look for the good and point it out in an honest way. That is helpful feedback. Celebrate often! Practice is hard work; finding moments of progress and making a huge deal of them is often the fuel that keeps us going.

In a recent workshop I facilitated for teachers, this topic came up and we all agreed another good way to think of this, especially to change our tone from a negative one, is to try giving neutral feedback. We don't have to gush with positivity at every moment, and maybe our child doesn't care for that kind of feedback anyway, but we can point out what is going on in a neutral way. Taking the emotion out of it, especially when it comes from parent to child, can really help. I want my child to focus on improving their skills in these moments rather than worry if they're making me happy. Neutral feedback is a good way to do that.

In the practice room with our children, avoid overly negative feedback. It can start to feel unmotivating or affect our interest in our instrument if all our flaws are detailed out to us on a daily basis. Negativity can be interpreted and internalized as "I can't do this" or "I'll never get it right."

Also, when our child is older and has to practice on their own, we want them to be telling themselves constructive things that help them improve instead of getting caught in negative thought patterns. I certainly don't want to feel that I have trained my child to have a stream of negative self-talk going on in their head when they practice alone. Changing our approach to a neutral or positive one when working with children helps counteract that tendency.

Feedback is a big part of being in any creative endeavor. It doesn't go away when students get older and start practicing independently. Rather, it starts to happen in our child's head for themselves. And of course, it happens with teachers, conductors, and ensembles they may participate in. Professional musicians play and give themselves feedback all the time. My goal as a parent is to help that feedback be constructive and to help my child move forward so their inner voice as they get older helps them instead of becoming a voice that is critical and paralyzing. I am not creating or 100 percent responsible for that inner voice, but I am heavily influencing it as it develops and want to treat that responsibility with a healthy respect.

Questions Are Key

A great strategy I would like to add to the list is question asking. If practice is simply an adult dictating things to a child, which they obediently follow without input or question, there may not be much conflict; but also, that child might not be mentally engaging in the process very much. I want to teach critical thinking skills. I want to teach the ability to break down a problem into small pieces *and* come up with solutions for improvement.

One of the best ways I've seen to make that happen is by asking questions, such as:

- What did your teacher want you to work on in that spot?
- Was your rhythm correct there?
- What were you watching while you played?
- What story can you tell with your music? Or what mood do you want to share?

Sometimes when I ask students questions like this in their lesson, they give me a blank look. Maybe they were lost in the music and not thinking about anything in particular. Maybe they were watching birds out the window or thinking about what's for dinner. When this happens, I simply ask them to play it again and give them a prompt for what to focus on. As a young student, I often had a lot of feelings when I was playing that I didn't know how to articulate or put into words. Having discussions with teachers, practice partners, and their students helps us put those feelings, and our own thought processes, into words so we can think more clearly about them.

Sometimes when students are particularly sensitive to the feedback from their parent, asking questions can be a great way to have a conversation about how something went, rather than for the child to feel like they're playing and then having judgment handed down from someone they would rather be getting approval from.

Playing an instrument can feel really personal. For some students, hearing feedback from a parent about how something "isn't there yet" just feels like too much of a personal attack no matter how we phrase it and no matter what our intentions. Self-assessment and discussions may be more productive.

I also want to acknowledge that some students truly do want blunt feedback and will ask for it. Take your cues from your student and adjust accordingly, but err on the side of a more gentle approach until you know what works for them.

Being able to use all these different strategies to give feedback and not fall into a role of pointing out mistakes helps our children make progress and feel supported in the process. I highly recommend starting with nonverbal feedback if you don't know which one to incorporate first, and especially if giving feedback has become stressful or full of conflict.

In my experience, a couple weeks of practice with some of these strategies that fit your child and their needs will help them start to relax and enjoy the process more. I hope this helps you if you're having a similar struggle.

ACTION STEPS

- Pick one of these approaches to feedback to try in practice this week.
- Reflect on how you like to receive feedback through work, music, or any other area of life. Realize your child may be the same or very different in what works for them.
- It may be clear right away if something doesn't work; other strategies may need time and experimentation to implement.

CHAPTER SIXTEEN

Ending with the Beginning in Mind

ISN'T PRACTICE JUST OVER WHEN YOU RUN OUT OF TIME OR GET TO the end of your assigned tasks? Maybe so, but ending our practice in an intentional way that helps build motivation can be an important consideration when we plan and help with practice sessions at home.

One of author Gretchen Rubin's secrets to adulthood is "The opposite of a great truth is also true," and I like to think about how this applies to practice.[1] How we start our practice sessions has a huge impact on how practice goes and how it ends.

I discovered this strategy quite by accident. When I first started practicing with my daughters, we had some less-than-ideal ends to our practice sessions. There was even an incident when a bow was thrown across the room in frustration, much to my horror, which I describe in more detail in *Beyond the Music Lesson.* It was one of those moments when I knew something had to change, and I set out to learn all I could about home practice and making it better.

There were times I thought we should "just do it a few more times" that backfired, in a dramatic way like this. Back then, I certainly didn't think about strategically ending with something my kids enjoyed when we first started to practice together, but I did learn over time what a benefit that was to us when it happened by accident.

A few times when I was just at the end of my patience and wanted my children to do one more task in practice, I would pick something light and easy, or ask them to pick something they loved and play it. It seemed like the easy way out of the end of practice from my perspective, but over time, I came to see that it was actually the best way for us to leave the end of a practice feeling calm and accomplished. It wrapped a nice bow around a practice session and made it feel good, even with its less-than-perfect moments in the middle. It's been one of my favorite tips ever since.

Why Ending with Purpose Helps

How we end our practice deserves some time and attention because the feeling we leave the practice room with is often the same feeling that comes to mind when it's time to start again tomorrow.

If we do any activity today that leaves us energized and excited about what we accomplished, we are much more likely to want to do it again. Compare that with an activity that leaves us feeling discouraged and overwhelmed. I'm not going to be as excited to start that activity again tomorrow.

Most parents want their child to be motivated to practice on their own one day, and it's hard to be motivated to do something that's associated with bad feelings, overwhelm, or arguments. That doesn't mean those things will never come up in practice; many times, they can't be avoided. However, even if there are challenging moments, we can choose to cap things off with something that reminds us of what we can do well, or what we love about playing our instrument. We can be intentional about ending with something positive or motivating on purpose.

Young Beginners

An important question I ask families, especially of new beginners, is "Did the practice end before your child asked it to?" I often teach preschoolers and I have found that if we keep practice short and stop before our child is begging to stop, it's so much easier to build their enthusiasm and motivation.

Of course, some children may always ask when practice will be over. Young children are still developing their concept of time, and it often helps them to see a written or picture list of the practice routine so they understand that practice will in fact end, and here's what we'll do first. We have a very concrete view of time as adults that young children have not developed yet.

Being clear about what tasks we're planning to do—and that once we do them, we're done—can help young children feel like this is a short activity rather than an endless one. That helps them feel more willing to work with us.

A simple way to communicate this is to create a picture for each task and have the activities mapped out visually. We can then talk about the next one and how many are left as we move through our practice time.

For young beginners, I work with what might include a picture of a bow, a violin, hands for clapping rhythms, and perhaps one other activity at the most. Then if one of my children feels restless and wonders how much time is left, we can visually show them ("There are two pictures left!").

Depending on a young child's attention span, you may need to divide up the tasks in a couple small practices or add in an intentional break. With young beginners, I want to start with assignments and expectations that fit the attention span the child has and then build from there. We want to work with our child's capabilities and at the same time trust that they will grow and so will their attention span with time.

When we see our time, our list of tasks, or our ability to focus coming to a close, that can be a signal to us to move to our ending activity. The younger the student is, the more I'm gauging when practice is over by cues from them that they're at the end of their ability to focus, although this is an important consideration even for adults.

Independent Practicers

For students who are grade school age and older, and who may be practicing on their own, having a conversation with your teacher about how much time to spend in practice is very important. If it feels like your child is begging to stop practice, but you haven't gotten through everything yet, that tells us we may need to adjust our approach.

Practicing in smaller chunks of time with breaks can be really helpful for students of all ages. Building in mini breaks into a longer practice session can help us stay focused and ensure we use our time well. In her book *Social Emotional Learning*, Marilee Sprenger writes, "If the brain focuses for too long, it gets tired, which leads to mind wandering or daydreaming. Focused attention for most students is somewhere between 5 and 10 minutes."[2] This isn't to say your practice is over after five or ten minutes, but you may want to build in a break and then get back to work.

The thing I know for sure is that we want to work with our brains and bodies to have healthy practice sessions. Pushing through and past our ability to focus a little bit can help us grow and improve. However, going too far can be counterproductive. If your teacher asks you to practice for thirty to forty minutes a day, that doesn't mean you can't break that up into smaller chunks of time throughout the day. You can go back to Chapter Twelve, all about planning practice, if you need some reminders about ways to do this.

Alternately, your child may need to dedicate more time to practice in order to complete their assignments. Ask your teacher how long they recommend practicing each day for your child's age and level. Consider increasing practice by five minutes at first and slowly adjusting.

For older students, likely practice will end when they either run out of time or get to the end of their assignments. Then it's time to have an ending activity in mind to wrap things up.

Picking a Strategic Ending Activity

My best suggestion is to end practice with something your child enjoys playing. For some students, this will be playing something easy that went really well earlier in the practice. For others, it's their note-reading assignment or figuring out a piece by ear. Some students crave unstructured time to noodle around or improvise on their instrument, and as long as they're old enough to treat the instrument with care, you may be able to let them do that as a "practice dessert" of sorts on their own. The main thing is to notice what your child loves and strategically bring it out at the end, like a treat at the end of practice time.

My goal is for students to leave the practice space feeling like they enjoyed that last thing they just did. I hope they feel accomplished or proud of their progress. Hopefully, they grow to enjoy other parts of practice too, but at least we can aim for one consistent, daily positive. Very strategically, we'll put it at the end of our time together in the practice room so we leave feeling good about our practice. That's a feeling we want to carry with us to tomorrow's practice. At the very least, it's something we can talk about and reconnect with to remember there are parts of the process we enjoy.

There's a famous saying: "Begin with the end in mind." In this case, we're doing the exact opposite. We want to end today's practice with tomorrow's practice in mind. What will leave us motivated? What can we schedule earlier in the practice when we have more mental energy so if we come up against frustration, it's not the last thing we did on the instrument that day?

We're not trying to have perfect practice every day, but we are trying to plan how we'll structure things for days when everything goes according to plan.

It's tempting to think about how great something will sound if our child just repeats it five more times. Or if the practice has gone well, we try to extend it longer and get more done, accidentally pushing too far. I understand that feeling when it seems that if our child is focused, we should keep it going for as long as possible. Depending on our child, that might work fine, but it might also backfire. Until we learn to read the signals, there's a danger of pushing too far, leading our children to shut down, feel overwhelmed, or be pushed past their ability to focus. This is important to notice.

Before we ever get to that point, it's far more valuable to make note of where to pick up tomorrow and to stop a little earlier than we may think we should have to. We can switch gears instead to an activity our child enjoys before we get to that state of meltdown or overwhelm. This way, we don't sabotage our efforts and we don't get in the way of our child coming back tomorrow to get to work again.

Learning the instrument is a long-term process. There will be more time to practice. We don't need to, and literally cannot, get to it all today. Being consistent and staying engaged in manageable chunks, which we'll talk more about in the next chapter, will help us reach our goals over time.

My biggest goal for young students is for them to develop a lifelong love of music, and I always want to be careful not to damage its development along the way. Endless practices causing overwhelm and frustration can do that if we're not careful.

Here are some ideas I've heard parents and practice partners use to cap off their practice positively:

- Play a favorite piece from earlier in the practice session.
- Note reading.
- Learning a piece with music and note-reading skills from a movie or just for fun.
- Giving a performance in different rooms of the house.
- Learning a piece by ear.
- Performing for pets, family members, or stuffed animals.
- "Noodling" on the instrument: play their own creations and explore the sounds it makes.

ACTION STEPS

- Reflect on how you are currently ending practice sessions in your house.
- Take note of the mood at the end. Even a fist pump in the air and a "Yes, I'm done!" that's accompanied by a smile counts as positive in my book.
- Notice which activities help your child tie a nice bow around the end of practice and leave the practice room feeling accomplished or satisfied. Do more of that on a regular basis to end your practices.

CHAPTER SEVENTEEN

Reflecting on Results in Practice

OUR FINAL PHASE OF THE PRACTICE CYCLE FOCUSES ON THE RESULTS we're getting in the practice room. The whole point of practice is to improve and make things easier. If we take one single day out of context, sometimes our results are hard to see. I recommend reflecting on each practice a bit, but also taking time to look back over the past month, quarter, and year from time to time to see how far your child has come.

I love this quote from world-class violinist Hilary Hahn reminding us how small bits of progress add up over time: "Even if you only make one small improvement a day, that's 365 points of improvement in a year."[1] We can end up with huge gains and results over time, from small daily steps forward.

Hopefully, we're always learning and growing, whether it's in these tiny daily increments or by big growth spurts that take us by surprise. It's sometimes easier to see our growth when we look back and over the past six months or a year. Then it might be more obvious how far we've really come through our daily work in the practice room.

Sometimes when we're the ones doing the daily work, or helping our child with it, it can feel like we're not making progress. Our progress might be happening in tiny steps forward that are hard to see from one day to the next. For example, I can often see little increments of progress from week to week as a teacher that are harder for families to recognize. There are six days of work being represented that allow me to see progress in a different way.

Sometimes we find out we're actually not making much progress, and if that's true, then we may need a change. Putting in work but not making progress gives us information. We may need to make adjustments to allow more progress to happen. Some skills take many months, or even longer, to learn, and our teacher can give us that reality check too. Others may need more attention to detail, and then the progress will start to be visible. I believe we can take a healthy approach to all of this when we think of practice in four phases: plan, practice, reflection, and feedback. They work in a loop.

When we pay attention to each phase, they all work together to move us forward. We plan what to practice, we do the work, we reflect on our results, and we get feedback from our teacher. This cycle is repeated over weeks and months and years and helps us stay organized and get the support we need to improve.

If we don't ever take our time to pause and think about the results we're getting, we may not realize when a change of approach in our practice session is needed, or when we have moments of progress to celebrate.

Reflecting on Our Results from Practice

I suggest asking yourself if progress was made in any of the following areas:

- A piece of music got easier to play.
- A technical skill improved.
- A clearer, more beautiful sound was produced.
- Your child played with more expression or artistry.
- Your child was able to focus and concentrate longer (even if it's a short amount of time) while playing.

These are the questions I posed in the *Positive Practice* workbook. I clearly remember sharing my workbook with students in my studio when it first came out and talking through this section in a parent meeting. One parent loudly said "Oh!" when I talked through these questions. While they knew they were supposed to be putting in time practicing, seeing these questions clearly laid out was a light-bulb moment for them to think about what they were trying to accomplish during that practice. Before seeing these points laid out, "improve" was a murky, hard-to-define term for them. You may feel the same.

When we're thinking about giving our practice a makeover or simply building a productive habit of practice, we might want to define improvement at a more basic level. We may need to first think about how we work together productively or get ourselves in the mindset for practice each day. We may need to simply carve out practice and make it happen consistently in the first place.

The questions I listed above could feel like lofty goals if we're simply trying to get through practice or establish the habit. For beginners or those working to turn around their practice, perhaps a list like this is more appropriate:

- Did we practice today?
- Did we have a plan?
- Were we able to follow it? How far did we get?
- Did my child get started with practice without a fight or battle of wills?
- Which tasks did we finish?
- What didn't we get to and need to include tomorrow?

Start where you are and with the skills you are working to build. After your practice, simply check in and think about how it went. Did something improve? Did you try something that worked well? If so, jot it down so you remember to repeat that activity.

Reflection after practice will help us check in on how our instrument and practice skills are developing in tandem. Depending on what you're focusing on at the moment with your teacher, you may want to reflect on one or the other, or maybe both.

Are We Making Progress?

When the question comes up of "Have we made progress?" I like to ask practice partners to look back at the lesson notes from six months ago or a recital video from a year in the past. What is hard to see from day to day can often be seen more clearly from a short distance away. Maybe progress is slow. Or we've been looking for progress in a certain area, but really it's happening somewhere else.

It's often easy to see how far we have left to go when we're working on a long-term project like learning an instrument. We see performances or listen to recordings from professionals that are inspiring and help us learn. Sometimes they also make it obvious how far we still have to go. We may see a huge gap between where we are now and where we want to be.

Sometimes, that gets discouraging. I find that practice partners who are musicians see this gap very distinctly and can get more easily frustrated with the process. I've also had students as young as four who can hear very clearly how they want to sound and find it very hard to tolerate the difference between that and how they sound right now as a beginner.

My favorite way to think about this comes from a concept from Dan Sullivan's work called The Gap and The Gain.[2] Sullivan is a business coach for high achievers, and he points out that we can measure our progress from two perspectives: the gap between where we are and where want to be or by how far we've come.

I first learned about this concept from reading an article by Dr. Benjamin Hardy, and this quote stuck out to me: "If you're growing but constantly measuring where you are against your ideal, you'll never get there. This will lead you to always feeling dissatisfied with yourself, which isn't helpful to your future goals and it robs you of the joy of the distance you've made."[3]

Sometimes, we can't help but see the gap. I think it's helpful to see what's possible and be inspired by it. The danger comes if we are focused there alone or can't appreciate our own progress because we're not there yet. Thinking about how far we've come is so powerful. Depending on our children's ages, they may not have the maturity to do this for themselves, but we, the adults practicing with them, certainly can. We can point out small bits of progress. We can make mini goals and celebrate them. We can stop measuring our child's progress by the gap, which may cause frustration, and start to measure and focus on our gains instead.

One way to do this is by making a list of all the new skills your child has learned in the last few months. Ask your child to come up with a list of what they think should be added. Ask your teacher if they can help give perspective as well. Sometimes, looking for the progress helps us see what was already there. That can be a powerful, motivating force as well.

I'm not suggesting we lower our standards or stop looking toward inspiring performers we want to emulate. But I do think we need to put our emotional energy and focus toward what's improving and celebrating the little steps along the way. This is the fuel for continued interest in improvement and our feeling of staying motivated.

Defining Our Results

The other thing we want to be careful of is not defining our "results" in too narrow of terms. We can fall into a habit of measuring results based on the number of pieces we've learned or where we are in a certain book, or series of books. That's certainly one way to measure progress, but there are so many other ways to measure how far we've come.

Knowing a piece of music and having the technical skills to play it well are two different things. How we play is probably even more important than *what* we play if we're measuring our progress in the practice room.

It's a shame to feel defeated or like we're not accomplishing anything, when in fact we might just be measuring the wrong thing, or too few things.

I encourage you to find new ways to measure progress. For example, we have a celebration each time a student graduates a book level in my studio—it represents a huge accomplishment. But for every book graduation, we have a hundred small celebrations along the way. Let's think more about some of the things we might forget to measure.

The Little or Invisible Signs of Progress

When I was young, I loved books that had a little hidden character to find throughout the pages. The little mouse in *Goodnight Moon* or the little worm in Richard Scarry books are two that I found delightful to look for. I loved searching through the bigger, more obvious pictures on the page and finding the little things that others might miss.

I feel like I still do that in my job now. I'm always looking for the little things that show us we've made progress when it's tempting to only notice and pay attention to the big ones. Sometimes, progress is big and dramatic. But many times, it's so small we might miss it if we don't look closely enough.

I started thinking about this after listening to artist Andy J. Pizza talk about how he got started on his series of art based on what he calls "invisible things."[4] He talked about how as a child he loved the things left to his imagination in picture books. He liked how his mind had to fill in what wasn't there. I'm a huge fan of all his work, but especially around this topic. When I first heard him talk about this and saw his artwork of invisible things where he has quirky cartoon characters of things like hope, time, patience, and fear, it made me think about all the invisible things that happen in music and in practice.

Some of the invisible things we see developing in practice and should celebrate include:

- the ability to focus
- motivation
- perseverance
- leadership
- fine motor skills development
- brain development

These skills are absolutely critical for advanced musicians to develop their playing and performance skills to a high level. Many of them are needed to learn to play at any level.

Sometimes we take these things for granted. They're hard to measure and remember to pay attention to. Other times, we may feel discouraged that it's taking a long time to learn to play a piece of music when really amazing things are happening in these other, less visible areas. If we look for what invisible things are improving, and celebrate them, we can see how much progress is actually being made.

I will never get tired of teaching a young beginner "Twinkle, Twinkle, Little Star" or leading a music class for babies where they get to dance with egg shakers for the first time. Because right in front of me, these huge leaps forward in thinking, moving, feeling, and being human are happening—things not everyone gets to learn how to do. Skills that need time, encouragement, and a positive environment to flourish in.

You, the practice partner at home, get to do this work too. Let's agree together to focus on the gain. We know the gap is there. We know "Twinkle, Twinkle, Little Star" isn't a professional violinist's concerto, but we are helping our children gain the first steps along the way. Whether or not they become professional musicians or play their instrument for the rest of their lives, they are gaining lifelong skills and I hope a lifelong love of music. The gain is where the motivation happens. Let's watch for and encourage even the tiniest bits of progress we see so our children can build on them.

The Practice Relationship

The last aspect of measuring our results I want to mention has to do with our practice relationship. Earlier in this book, we talked about the high percentage of practice partners who reported that the parent-child relationship, and navigating all the challenges that come up, was their biggest struggle with music practice.

As practice partners, we want the practice to be done as efficiently and productively as possible. I know I did. I think it's also important to look beyond that, though, and really think about what helps our child practice *well.* We can't control if our child comes into the practice room feeling tired, frustrated about other things, or just not in the mood to practice on any given day.

None of that is our responsibility. But we do get to set the tone for practice and influence many parts of it, as we've been discussing in the last few chapters. We can help our children feel understood, that their needs are respected, and that we are there to help them as they learn the assignments for their teacher.

We can think about if we're injecting fun into the practice and keeping it in balance with the hard work to be done. Fun for your child might be checking off boxes or playing a game as part of the day's practice. We can think about what sets up the right environment for our child to focus and get work done.

I appreciate that it's not always easy to keep all of this in mind. Certainly, practice with our children is one of many responsibilities on our list for any given day. Sometimes, it feels like our particular child, or the dynamics between us, makes practice challenging.

I can very honestly tell you that's how I felt, and that's exactly why I do the work I do now to help practice partners like you navigate their practice sessions more positively. We can't guarantee there won't be struggles or conflict, but we can think about the relationship we cultivate in the practice room and the impact it has on our child's love of music.

Just like we might have read to them when they were young and cuddled in our laps, we can make the practice room a place for warm connection with one another so our child is in the best frame of mind for learning to practice and for working hard. We want them to associate music more with positive feelings than negative ones.

ACTION STEPS

- Set aside a few moments to reflect on the results you're seeing in practice.

- Ask your teacher if you're unsure about the rate of progress your child is moving at, or if there's anything you can do to improve your results on the instrument.

- Together with your child, spend more time focused on how far you've come and on remembering all you've learned.

- Look for the tiny and invisible ways progress might be happening right in front of you.

SECTION THREE

How to Make Practice Work for *Your* Child

CHAPTER EIGHTEEN

Build a Practice Toolkit

When we're young musicians, often a toolkit of physical items and motivational aides can make a huge difference in our practice sessions. As students get older, our needs shift and it's helpful to think of having a toolkit of strategies we can pull from to practice effectively. Let's talk about both so you can decide what meets your child's needs right now.

Alan Duncan, the father of a thirteen-year-old violinist, shared this about how having a practice toolkit: "The concept of having everything close at hand is so appealing, because it means fewer interruptions. And having things available is a constant reminder to use them!"

Why I Recommend a Practice Toolkit

When a new family starts lessons in my studio, one of the tasks I give in the first few weeks of lessons is starting to build a practice toolkit. I often start young beginners between the ages of three to eight, for context. Experience has taught me that for this age group, some days practice flows easily. On these days, families can potentially go down the list of practice tasks and get things done without much fanfare.

More often than not, though, we really need ways to support and expand focus in our practice. We need some creative ways to keep our child engaged in the practice session and keep things fun and creative. If we're the musician practicing, we may need some extra tools to keep *ourselves* engaged. Older students might need strategies to pull from in the practice room as they learn how to practice effectively.

If we wait until one of these days that needs creativity and extra strategies, and *then* pause our practice session to go find some ideas that work, it's often too late. Our child's attention might be already gone for the day, and we have to restart tomorrow instead.

This is why having an already assembled practice toolkit is so helpful. Before a day like this happens, we gather supplies that can be used in practice and keep them right in our practice space. This collection of practice items is something I ask families to gather from around the house at first, then it can be added to and supplemented with new items over time.

There are number of places you can store your tools for practice. You might have a side table drawer, a music bag where you keep your materials, or you may want to use a pencil pouch or Ziploc bag to keep your practice toolkit items in.

"I keep mine in a clear plastic storage container so I can easily see what I'm looking for," says teacher Cheryl Edwards Ludwig. She adds, "Another teacher I know uses a tackle box. The kids love seeing what I pull out of my box to use for repetitions and games." You can take this idea and make it your own at home and add this same kind of mystery and excitement to practice.

The Young Musicians Practice Toolkit

The primary goals for having a practice toolkit for young students is to help us make practice more fun and engaging, while actually making progress on our assignments. It can help us increase the number of repetitions our child is willing to do with a little extra planning and a few items from around the house gathered in advance. As I'm writing this chapter, I have a whole bag full of items in front of me that I often use in lessons for these purposes. If you're helping a young musician practice, I suggest you find similar items around the house to put into your own practice toolkit.

Some of the items we might include are:

1. Small finger puppets: I put these on the end of the bow, use them to give instructions to students who think it's more fun to hear "Let's play that again!" from a small, blue hippo than from me, and use them for helping students develop small muscle control by putting them on fingers while we sing.

2. Little erasers shaped like animals: These are fun for balancing on string instruments, putting on the white keys of the piano to find specific notes, and especially moving from one end of a table to another after segments of practice as we count repetitions.

3. Practice dice: We can roll dice to see how many times to repeat something; we can assign a different number to each of our practice tasks and roll to decide the order of practice; and we can come up with any number of creative games or game boards to use with dice with a little of our own creativity.

4. Small coins or rocks: I love these for counting and for balancing on hands to work on our hand shape. They can even be used as a marker for a game of music bingo or music tic-tac-toe.

5. A practice chart or 3-by-5 card: Office supply stores often sell fun rewards charts that you can add stickers to, mark off, or fill in the boxes on as days of practice or practice tasks are completed. Sometimes, I will assign a student to fill one up specifically for a certain piece of music I want them to very carefully repeat over a few weeks. Other times, families say a 3-by-5 card that can be marked or drawn on is just as motivating.

6. Stickers: These can be great fun for students of all ages, and there are endless options. Find a good place to stick them during practice: a 3-by-5 card, a chart, on your child's shirt, on a poster in the practice space, or any other spot you choose. Seeing the stickers add up can be very motivating!

7. Rhythm instruments: Inexpensive options like wooden sticks, wooden spoons, egg shakers, a plastic tub with a lid for a drum, or whatever else you might have around the house are fun ways to practice rhythm and have some free, creative movement between more disciplined tasks on an instrument.

8. Sand timers: I have sand timers that are set up for a specific length of time: two, three, and five minutes, for example. These can be a great way to stick with an activity for a set amount of time or to create a challenge to see if a task can be done well for a whole minute, which is where I would recommend starting.

9. Bead counters: There are a few great options of companies that make these, like The Practice Shoppe and The Enchanted Workshop, and I have heard of families

> making their own as well. Beads are connected by a string or wire and moved from one side to another as tasks or repetitions are completed. This is really motivating for many students, and it's self-contained, so everything stays together in one place.

I hope that helps get you started. Really, any little items you have around the house that your child finds fun to engage with will probably work with a little creativity.

Having a way to count repetitions for practice tasks and make them fun and enjoyable is often the best way to get more done during practice time with young students. It can help us repeat things many more times, with less resistance, and is priceless for days when we just need a little extra motivation to keep working.

Using the Practice Toolkit to Build Focus

A lot of what we do in the early stages of learning how to practice involves stringing together tiny moments of focus. We turn this string of little moments of concentrated work into a longer practice session by building in short breaks and then getting back to work.

Practice might start as short as five minutes but will grow over time. Your assignments will increase and so will your child's ability to string together more of these focused chunks of work in the practice room.

Building in a little break to move a small item, add a sticker to a chart, or roll the dice helps us insert a strategic break in between these small, focused moments. These breaks are key for students of all ages; they just start to space out more as students are able to focus for longer bursts of time.

Marilee Sprenger, an expert on the brain and learning, shares the importance of helping the brain to focus again by adding novelty and breaking up our predictable routine.[1] She recommends any activity for these brain breaks that helps us wake up the part of the brain that makes choices if incoming information should be acted on or ignored, especially activities that involve some sort of movement.[2]

For some students, a movement break is going to be vital for them to focus well during practice. Walking around the house or up and down the stairs is one option. Jumping jacks or somersaults work as well. Jumping on a mini trampoline if you have one (without the instrument, please!) is a fun option too.

Research shows that moving our bodies helps us integrate new information, access the part of our brain that helps us learn and make rational decisions, and get back to a calm emotional state so our brains and bodies can work together. In their book, *The Whole-Brain Child*, Dr. Daniel Siegel and Dr. Tina Payne Bryson share the story of a young child who was overwhelmed by homework and how running around his neighborhood helped him. "So, after his run, his body sent 'calmer' information to his upstairs brain, meaning that his emotional balance returned and different parts of his brain and body began to function again in an integrated way."[3]

If we think back to our myth of the lone, focused practicer, you can see this approach is the exact opposite. Often, movement helps our brain and body work together. Insisting a child stand still during practice can actually be quite counterproductive. While this can be true of musicians of all ages, young children especially need this opportunity to move in their practice sessions.

Some students, such as those with a diagnosis of ADHD, may need to incorporate movement into their practice indefinitely. While I was writing this book, I often went out for walks when I felt like I just couldn't focus any longer, and I do the same for my own music practice. Other students will need a lot of movement like this at certain points in their development more than others.

Our practice toolkit for young musicians can incorporate many fun items that help us count, build in brain breaks, and use creativity to make practice more engaging and effective. We can also incorporate and plan for some creative ways to move. This type of plan of action, and the tools you have gathered, will help keep students working productively in a way that keeps their interest and helps them thrive and learn.

A Practice Toolkit for Older Students

As our children get older and start to practice more independently, they may not need these tiny items to count or dice to roll. On average, I would say this happens around ages eleven to thirteen; however, there are exceptions. Teens may still find some of the previous ideas fun or helpful for focus, in which case, use what works! I know grown adults who roll dice and use timers for practice. I also recently saw a social media post by a composer who was moving small, beautiful stones from one dish to another as part of her own practice routine. We should respect what our student needs to practice effectively regardless of age.

With all that in mind, what we can say with confidence that students need as they get older and more advanced is a toolkit of practice strategies to use when practicing.

When professional musicians practice, they often play a section of their music, decide what they want to improve, and then scroll through a mental checklist they have of different strategies that might work to accomplish their goal.

The biggest complaint I get from families of newly independent practicers is that the student wastes time or doesn't know what to practice. They might play straight through their music over and over and don't make as much progress as everyone would like.

My theory is that this is because they are missing, or haven't yet developed, that mental checklist that professionals have already that includes strategies for how to work on their assignments. Sometimes we assume students have picked it up by working with their families in practice or with their teacher in a lesson, but often we need to be more clear and direct than that.

The exciting thing is that practice is more fun and engaging for many students once they learn to do it effectively. I recently had a conversation with Dr. Molly Gebrian, a professional violist who teaches at the University of Arizona and specializes in music and the brain, and she shared her own experience with learning how to practice:

> Once you know how to practice well, then you really start to see improvement. The issue for me growing up was that I didn't know how to practice *well.* And so I wasn't getting much better because I wasn't practicing—I was playing through. In retrospect, that's why it felt like a frustrating waste of time. Once I learned how to practice well, then I could see my improvement and then practicing was suddenly something I wanted to do.[4]

This is what we want for our children and students. We want them to truly understand how to improve their skills through effective, meaningful practice rather than playing straight through. Having strategies that work is a big part of this.

I suggest creating a physical list with your practice strategies. It could be on a device in digital form or handwritten and then kept in the practice notebook. But what we want to have is a list of strategies we know will work when we're practicing a difficult section. We want to have something to reference that jogs our memory about the different ways we can approach a practice assignment.

Some of the strategies I hope my students start adding to their list include:

1. Practicing slower: A common theme for my students is rushing through, which makes it hard to hear if we have played correctly or have actually fixed anything. I like to talk about playing at a "thinking speed" when learning new music.

2. Practicing one hand at a time: Musicians often have complicated and very different tasks assigned to each hand on our instrument. Isolating and practicing one at a time helps us find where we need to focus our efforts and to think clearly about what each hand is doing at any given moment.

3. Practicing with a metronome: I can't emphasize this enough. Sometimes the only way to really slow ourselves down in practice is to play with the help of a metronome. Other times, we're working to increase our tempo and the metronome can help us with that as well. Talk to your teacher about good speeds to work with if you aren't sure where to start.

4. Practicing with a drone: A drone is a sustained, or held-out, note on one pitch. Practicing with a drone can help us notice when we need to work on our pitch. It can help us hear if our scales are in tune. Many tuning apps also act as

a drone, but my favorite to use are cello drones, which can be found by searching online. You'll want to find a drone in the key of the music or scale you are working on. Again, ask your teacher for details if you're unsure.

5. Practicing through active listening: Here, the student looks at their music and follows the score while they listen to the piece being performed at a high level. This helps us hear what we're aiming for and how it relates to what we're seeing on the page. Professionals use this strategy too. It really helps!

Your teacher might assign you a specific strategy and send you home to work on it. Not only should you do that, but if it worked for you, I would add it to the list that you are collecting. You might hear a great strategy in a master class, or at a workshop you attend, or from an orchestra director.

Being on the lookout for these strategies and keeping a record of them to reference is very valuable. Not every strategy works in every situation, but if we have a list of strategies that work for *some things, some of the time*, we can start to make educated choices about how we might practice. Then we move past the ineffective strategy of playing through but not improving anything.

If we can see that something does need improving in our practice session, but we're not sure where to start, we can pull out this list of practice strategies and pick something to try. They can get us started at the very least. Our strategy list keeps us from blankly staring at the stand and from wasting time.

I'm hoping by the time my students are practicing independently that they at least have a short list of these strategies to draw from. Putting together your list of practice strategies is a great way to help independent practice become more productive.

If your child is old enough to be practicing on their own, they likely are old enough to pick from the list what they think will help them with practice or ask their teacher which strategy is best.

Just like the list of ideas for younger students, we want effective ways to help us stay focused, keep it fun and engaging, and make improvements in our playing. We don't want to spend valuable practice time searching for them when we're stuck, though; we want to have them gathered up close by and ready to use.

Starting with some of the ideas in this chapter and then adding to them as you find what appeals to your child and what your teacher suggests can really help the daily work of practice be more effective and engaging. This is when our work can feel exciting and productive, which helps everyone with their motivation in the practice room just like Dr. Gebrian shared.

I love this reflection on the changing nature of a practice toolkit over time by Alan Duncan, the parent of a thirteen-year-old violinist: "How our practice toolkit has changed over time! Early on, it was materials for games and distractions—dice, tokens, etc. Now it's mostly materials for marking up music—a variety of highlighters (including our new favorite: erasable highlighters), special pencils, and a recent addition of transparent Post-it notes, which are great for temporary markings."

ACTION STEPS

- Identify if your student could use a practice toolkit of physical items, ways to incorporate movement, practice strategies, or some combination.

- Find items from around the house to use in practice to extend focus and put them together in one place, in your practice area.

- Remember we are working to make practice more enjoyable, productive, and effective. Even if what works for your child seems very different than what you pictured, if it's accomplishing these goals, please don't worry.

- Talk with your teacher if you have any questions about what tools or strategies fit in with the age and level of playing your child is at.

CHAPTER NINETEEN

Practice Personalities

As we think about working with the unique needs of the child in front of us in the practice room, one of the best ways to help is to learn the unique ways *they* learn and focus best. Some of this, as we've discussed before, is discovered through trial and error while we learn to practice together. We become a student, in a way, of what works in practice with each of our children, and we often learn very clearly what doesn't work. Our approach to practice can shift in both big and subtle ways to meet our child's needs and help them thrive.

As a practice partner, we don't have to go into this process without any information to help us get started. There are many great resources and frameworks for thinking about the way students practice and about personality in general. A couple that I love and highly recommend are Michelle Horner's book, *Life Lens: Seeing Your Children in Color*, and Gretchen Rubin's framework of *The Four Tendencies.*

For me, resources like these are not about trying to label students or put them into boxes. What I'm looking for are all the strategies that come along with such resources.

Even if we aren't totally sure where our child fits into one of these models, or we feel like they fit into multiple categories, or we don't like putting them in a category at all, we can still use the different strategies recommended as a menu of ideas to pull from. In our practice sessions, we can try out some of the suggested strategies to see if it helps us practice together more effectively.

We can also help students think about how they learn best. That way, they can eventually practice effectively on their own with more information about how to work with themselves. If you have a teen who is already practicing independently, they might think about how the information in this chapter applies to them, right now, and how they might use it to help themselves practice more effectively.

In my book *Beyond the Music Lesson*, I suggest a few practice personalities that pull together a lot of the ideas I've gotten from the other frameworks and puts them into very simple terms to get you started. They don't have catchy names, but I do think they can help us start to find practice strategies that work for each child.

If this topic is interesting to you, I suggest you check out additional resources and other frameworks to think about it more deeply. We can never have too many strategies to help us think creatively about how to practice better whether we are practice partners, teachers, or students.

In my mind, there are four different practice styles, or personalities, that I see come up most often. Sometimes, they're easy to use to our advantage in the practice room; other times, we need to learn to work with them, or they get in the way of effective home practice.

I have defined the four practice personalities as:

1. self-directed
2. adult-directed
3. game-oriented
4. detail- or checklist-oriented

You may feel like your child falls into more than one of these categories, or even all of these at some point in their practice. What

I invite you to think about is what works for them best when there's a challenging assignment to practice that takes extra focus and motivation. Which strategy helps them to stay engaged and work hard in the music practice at that moment? That will be the key to helping improve practice, through increased focus and motivation, right away.

The important thing to know is which strategies to turn to when the going gets tough and we have to put in the most focused work. It's very possible when your child is a new beginner that one of these styles of practice works the best and that things will need to change over time based on their development and changing needs as a student.

That's why I suggest holding on to these categories loosely but still resolving to find what works right now. Let's talk about each one of them and how they might help us in the practice room.

Self-Directed Practice

Self-directed students tend to have more of an independent streak. Eventually of course, we want every student to be self-directed because they will practice independently one day. But some students need the ability to be more independent at an earlier age, I've found, or power struggles can start to happen in our practice sessions. In fact, not enough independence or ability to make choices in their practices might be counterproductive or demotivating for students like this.

It can be a challenge when a preschool student cannot complete the assignments they're given without help but are quite insistent they don't want or need any. We can work together to have some give-and-take in the practice room so that at least some of it is more under their control or gives them more choices for decision-making.

We want our children to engage their brain in practice and be highly motivated to get things done. The key is learning how to work with this style of practice and respecting the need for independence while also working as a team.

Sometimes, simply taking ourselves as a practice partner out of the equation when it comes to saying what we're going to do next helps the students a lot. We might roll the dice to tell us how many times to play something or use an app with a wheel that randomly chooses what we play next.

I have a colleague who sometimes writes all the tasks that need to be done on a whiteboard and then lets the student pick up the order and erase them when finished. We can also write tasks on a slip of paper and then scramble them up in a bowl to be fished out by the student one by one. We can still decide what will be practiced this way, but our child is choosing the order and feels more ownership and independence.

In an interview with Michelle Horner, author of the book *Life Lens,* she shares the strategy of having a finger puppet or stuffed animal tell a young child what to do. I love this idea because it takes some of the "this is personal" aspect out of the practice dynamic and can really help students who need to feel more ownership to be successful.

Giving self-directed students lots of choices is key, as you can see from all of these examples. As a parent, I never wanted to ask, "Do you want to practice today?"

That's not the kind of choice we're talking about, because I made a commitment to the daily practice routine and know how important consistency is. But choices, or random games of chance, about the order and how many times to play something are very appropriate for practice and keep things moving along so we can make progress.

My oldest daughter definitely fell into this self-directed category, and being self-directed has served her very well, which I can see very clearly now that she's in her midtwenties. Working with her in practice could be challenging at times, which we can both laugh about now. I had to learn to respect the fact that she needed choices to make and to find creative ways to let her make them.

We definitely worked better together once I stopped trying to fight her self-directed tendencies and instead worked with them so she could learn how to make choices within our practice sessions. Giving her more of a sense of being in charge, in appropriate ways, was really the best thing I could do in any part of her life to keep her motivated and working hard.

When I work with students who I know need to be more self-directed, I try to be very clear about which assignments need a practice partner's help, and which can be done more independently. Sometimes, I even tell the student that I'm assigning the helping task to their practice partner and I ask them to please allow that person to do their job and help. Sometimes, our teacher can help provide this extra support for us, if we ask.

Adult-Directed Practice

In contrast to the first practice personality, some students really like someone else guiding them through their practice session. I can usually tell who these students are, because when I try to make a fun review game in lessons and let them choose the next piece to play, their eyes get big and they stare at me like a deer in the headlights.

Clearly having to make these decisions is not fun or motivating for them. Eventually, every student needs to learn how to practice independently, and your teacher will work with your child on those skills over time. Students also tend to develop more confidence about independent practice over time as they gain more skills on the instrument and learn more practice strategies. They may always prefer someone help them outline practice, though, and there are resources for that even for professional musicians.

For now, though, it does make it simpler to lead our children through practice when they're perfectly happy to have us in this leading role. It can be challenging sometimes when we as the adults wish our children were more independent about their practice. My advice to practice partners is this: For now, if your child is a beginner especially, just try to feel comfortable being in the driver's seat of practice. Being in charge of every detail of practice is not forever, but it will make a world of difference in this point in time.

You may need to choose the order for everything in practice for your adult-directed practice sessions. If it makes it more fun for you, you can use some of the strategies from the last section and roll the dice or pull names for the next piece out of a jar or bowl. But it's okay to take the lead for now, knowing this won't last forever.

In the beginning stages, we're building motivation and getting through the practice tasks in front of us so we can build our skills. Using the fact that our child likes us to lead them in practice to our advantage, we can take note of what the teacher would like to happen in practice and help make that happen each day in the practice room.

As the practice partner, you may want to spend a little extra time preparing a plan for practice and what strategies to use to lead your child through their assignments if you're leading everything. Over time, your child can work with their teacher on these skills and will no doubt become more independent.

Game-Oriented Practice

While not every child is interested in playing games during a practice session, students who fall into this category are able to get a lot done in their practice when a game is involved. For some students, this helps the most for new music being learned. For others, the most helpful time to incorporate a game is when they're polishing or refining a piece that's not brand new anymore.

You can observe your child and notice at which point in the practice they might need this extra support or motivation.

Sometimes, it can be a challenge as practice partners when games don't appeal to us. That can make this a hard practice personality to navigate at first. Maybe we don't find them fun, or we just want to get on with it and get the practice tasks accomplished, or we feel like it takes too much time to get the game set up and it eats into our practice time.

If you simply don't find games appealing, but you can see they really help your child to focus longer and stay engaged, I encourage you to set that aside temporarily and shift your focus to what your child needs to learn their assignment.

It's important to remember that hard work can be disguised as a game. I have seen students who could only get through a couple repetitions of an assignment before a game was added into practice, but then be able to accomplish much, much more when they had the incentive of a game alongside the task.

We won't be practicing with our children forever, and they likely won't find games appealing forever in their practice, or at least they won't need us to implement them. This is a moment when we are giving the gift of our presence, attention, and working with our child's unique needs so they can practice successfully.

If we have a game-loving child who really can use them to help their focus, insisting they do an equal number of repetitions with no fun or games involved is likely going to make practice much more of a chore. I'm always thinking about building a love for music and working with what a child needs, and sometimes that comes with a little extra attention to practice strategies like these.

It helps keep practice from dragging out if we pick games where the rules are clearly defined and it doesn't take too long to set up and get started. Simple games work great, and more complicated games may have to be done outside of practice sessions. I think that's a great boundary to set.

Please note that we don't have to use a game for every part of the practice. I would pick the one part of practice that feels like the most work and incorporate the game into that.

Alternately, some families have a game that has more to do with how many tasks get done. For example, you might spin the game spinner one time to move on the game board for each task completed on the practice sheet. That's a great strategy too that helps us build in a brain break between each task on our list for the day.

There are endless music practice games available online if you do a search for them. We talked about some of them in our practice toolkit chapter as well. You may end up with a collection of ideas you'll want to rotate through.

One of my colleagues told me they use games so much in practice that they had a whole collection of them and would begin each practice day with her asking her child, "Which game should we use in practice today?" And this was their way of easing into the practice time together. The student chose the game, they got it ready to go, and then they got to work!

Detail- or Checklist-Oriented Practice

The final strategy, or practice personality, has everything to do with checking off boxes and following lists. Some students really love a practice chart with little boxes for each task they need to complete each day. It can feel very satisfying to go down the list and check off each completed task.

To help with this, I give out a practice sheet each week that has these boxes printed right on it along with our assignments handwritten in. Some of my students absolutely love this and find it very motivating. Others don't check the boxes off at all, or if I insist they do, it comes back with all the checkmarks looking exactly the same in the same color ink. I would bet it was all checked off in the car on the way to the lesson.

I've learned over time the checklist is great to offer as a tool but not to insist on, because for some people it's not motivating or useful at all. Maybe it's satisfying or helpful for you as a practice partner to have a checklist like this to work from, even if your child is uninterested. By all means, use one. Your practice personality is an important part of the equation too.

If your teacher doesn't give out a sheet like this, you can make your own in a spreadsheet or find one premade by searching online. One way you can support your child is by creating this checklist for them and putting it somewhere in plain sight during practice. They may need someone to talk them through the items on the list, and then they can put on their own sticker or checkmark as the task is completed.

As a sidenote, I often see a correlation between the students who love the details of the checklist and love to ask questions during their practice, because the details are motivating to them and help them care more about what they're learning. They may want to know about the composer, why we are being asked to do certain things a specific way, and endless other possibilities.

This can sometimes seem like a stalling tactic, and maybe sometimes it is. But I do find for these students, having a way to capture those questions and coming back to them can be very motivating.

You may want to consider a question limit for each practice. After your child has asked two or three questions that may be only somewhat related to the task at hand, they have to wait until after practice time. Or you can find a place to jot them down in the practice notebook and come back to them together later on. That could entail an internet search, a question to your teacher in the next lesson, or checking out some books about music or composers at the library.

The details are likely what your child finds motivating, so we can help connect them to how to find those details and feed their curiosity, and at the same time their motivation to keep learning and playing music.

Take a few moments and think about which of these types of practice you think applies to your child or children. Likely, if you have more than one child, they will each have their own unique practice style preference. I know in my case, I was tempted to use the strategies that worked for my older daughter and use them in practice with her sister. I quickly learned that I needed to start over and do the work to figure out what worked for my younger daughter as an individual. They were completely different in their approach to practice. Many parents of multiple children tell me they found the same thing to be true for them. Please consider each child in your family as an individual so everyone gets a chance to work with their strengths.

Ángel Falú-García shares this great example of how this kind of information helps us in lessons and home practice:

> As a violin teacher, understanding my students' personalities and learning styles not only helps me connect with them, but also, it's helped me guide parents in understanding their kids. An example that comes to mind was having a fast-pace parent understand that her child needed for her to slow

> down and allow more time to transition in and out of lessons and practice.
>
> Mom is a go-getter/no-nonsense type of person who likes to get things done fast. Her very sensitive and slow-paced boy, however, couldn't handle it. There were a lot of tantrums, and lessons were rough for a while. But once I helped Mom understand her kid's time awareness and slower pace, the tantrums subsided and starting practice got way easier and fun! Lessons have gone smooth as well.

Understanding what a student needs, whether that is a change of pacing or new strategies that help us focus, can make a world of difference. Simply reading these descriptions and thinking through the strategies can give us some aha moments about how to work better with one of our children in practice.

If you really aren't sure which one applies to your child, it's time to do some experimenting. Maybe as an easy way to start, pick the one that's most appealing to you as the practice partner. Or go with your hunch based on what you have observed so far about how they approach other activities. Just be sure to notice what truly helps your child practice at their best.

It's perfectly valid to rotate through all of these and then see what you find out. I do think that our child's practice personality can change over time and new strategies might be necessary to find if it does. Working to find the right balance for our child's need for getting input and developing as musicians helps us practice together and helps our children learn to work with themselves as they mature and grow.

ACTION STEPS

- ♪ Which of the four practice personalities do you think applies to you when learning something new?
- ♪ Which of them do you think applies to your child, who is learning to practice?
- ♪ What is one new idea you got from this chapter that you can add into practice this coming week?

CHAPTER TWENTY

Working with the Unique Needs of Your Child

ONE OF THE THINGS I LOVE ABOUT TALKING TO GROUPS OF PARENTS, and practice partners, all over the country in workshops and parent sessions is that I get to hear about all the creative ideas they find to keep their children engaged in practice. The ideas are endless. After twenty years of teaching, I still hear new creative takes on making practice work. This tells me how normal it is to need to find an approach that is the best fit for the unique needs of my own children.

Dr. Karin Hendricks shared this on the topic:

> No child is the same, and all children need different things to be successful, motivated, and fulfilled. So what works with one child may completely flop with another! That's where curiosity and wonder come in: If we approach children (and really everyone) with a sense of curiosity ("Hmmm, I wonder why . . . I wonder how . . ."), then we are open to finding new and exciting ways to engage with them. This also takes the pressure off the child—and the parent—to be perfect, or to fit some sort of ideal. That image of an "ideal child" is an unfortunate and hurtful myth.

We need to tailor advice and new ideas to our child's needs. That sense of curiosity and letting go of how things *should* look in the practice room can help us do just that.

In this book, we've discussed setting ourselves up for success, phases of a practice session, and many ideas to make practice easier. Now it's time to make a plan that works in our homes and practice rooms. It's time to think specifically about practice that works for your child and family.

It would be wonderful if, along with the instrument, we also got to start out music lessons with the exact combination it takes to motivate our particular child and make practice work. Instead, this is something we often find out by close observation and some trial and error. We learn over time what to put in our practice toolkit and what strategies related to practice personalities are a good fit. It gets easier. We can also learn a lot by hearing other parents share their own experiences with us, and taking what we can from their journey to help our own.

I recently asked practice partners in an online group I run what they learned about working with the unique needs of their child in practice. Here's what a few of them said:

> Different things work for different children. My kids all practice in very different ways, and different things motivate them. Pay attention to what works and go with it. Don't be afraid to change if it doesn't work anymore. Also, ask for what works for other people, but don't feel bad if it doesn't work for you or your child! As we say in my house, "Everyone likes different things!"
>
> —Jo-Anne Steggall

Follow your instinct. Count to five inside your head before counting to five out loud. Some days anything is good enough.

—Ainslie Jackel

Don't practice on an empty stomach! This goes for the parent and the child!

—Rebecca Lane

Parent and practice with the child in front of you, not who you expect them to be or how you expect them to behave.

—Tayva Singer

Get creative. Make sure that practice is fun. A small child will likely not perfect the bow hold after one lesson, much less one month, much less one year. But make sure they have fun during practice so they will be playing in one month and one year.

—Nitin Bhojraj

Allow all feelings (that doesn't mean allow all actions) and discuss them so you can create a safe space to learn!

—Kimberley Wong

He started at four and he wasn't able to practice straight for thirty minutes. He took karate breaks, milk breaks, ninja-fighting sword breaks, etc. in between practice for several years. I had to be very patient. He's more mature now and more willing to practice straight through. Every child is different. Find what works.

—Billie Rose Robles

As I shared at the beginning of this book, letting go of my ideas about what practice *should* look like and really paying attention to what my own children needed to practice well was what started to change everything for our family. These parents found ways to make practice work for them too.

You get to discover how to do the same for your children. We can start to do this by putting the ideas from this book into action and noticing what works well and what gets in the way of progress. We can give ourselves and our children grace when it's hard, or we need to find a new strategy.

We can help our child gain the skills needed for their instrument and help structure practice and make it happen in a way that takes into account how they learn and what motivates them. And if we're not sure what those things are, we can learn them along the way.

One important consideration about how to make practice work for your child is to keep their age and development in mind. Here are some of my favorite strategies to share with practice partners:

Early Childhood

The ideas below for music practice in the early childhood years apply roughly to students ages three to six. This is an age when play, creativity, and working with the developmental needs and interests of our child are absolutely vital. A focus on connection and building a love for music over primarily focusing on results is so important at this stage (although it's important for every age).

- **Games:** Children learn through play, and games help keep practice fun too.
- **Imagination:** Work with your child's imagination instead of against it.

- **Routine**: Getting into a routine helps your child learn what to expect and over time helps reduce resistance.

- **Creativity:** This is key. Keep things fun and bring in creative ideas that are interesting to your child outside of practice. Try new ideas! Even if they don't work, we have learned something about what strategies do work for our child.

- **Timing**: Older students can dig deep and focus on demand. Young children have times in their day when they can focus the best. Schedule practice with those needs in mind.

- **Focus on the positive**: Little improvements and moments of focus or progress are worth celebrating! Sometimes, we have to make a habit of looking for them and focusing on them as the practice partner, but doing so makes for a positive, encouraging practice environment.

- **Being present**: Especially in these early years, your help is needed in the practice room. Setting aside the time, staying engaged, and helping with the structure and learning tasks of practice is especially needed from adults at this age.

Grade School

These tips apply to students from about age six to twelve. Students at these ages need support in practice but also an opportunity to make decisions and be a part of planning practice so they can one day successfully practice on their own. Building a practice routine and learning *how* to practice before students become more independent is key.

- **Develop ownership**: Help your child connect to the instrument and process of practice in a personal way. Ask questions, let them make choices, and have independence where appropriate.

- **Be consistent:** Practice partners regularly report that skipping days actually makes it harder to practice the next day, so help structure practice and initiate practice when needed.

- **Help with getting started:** The start of practice can be a challenge. Find out what eases your child into practice and help them get started with a transition activity that eases their brain and body into practicing mode.

- **Make it social:** Motivation often comes from making music with others. Attend group classes or join an orchestra. Get together with a practice buddy. Look for social opportunities for musicmaking within your family, studio, or community.

- **Develop a practice habit**: Relying on our habits is more effective than using willpower or trying to remember to practice. Families I talk with report that making practice part of the daily routine is the number one thing that makes sticking with music lessons work for them.

- **Embrace your role as practice coach:** Helping with practice sometimes looks more like a give-and-take or teamwork situation as students get older and learn more practice skills. The help your child needs may shift and change. See what they need based on how involved your teacher would like you to be and how much support your child needs to successfully complete practice tasks. As assignments get more complex, help structuring practice, staying focused, and staying motivated are often most needed even if the notes and musical assignments start to become more independent.

The Teen Years

These ideas apply to students ages twelve to thirteen and up. A focus on increased independence and responsibility coupled with lavish amounts of encouragement and continued support where needed is key. Your supporting role changes in these years but stays important for your child's success.

- **Encourage:** The biggest thing your child needs from you during this time is encouragement. Sometimes this comes directly from us and sometimes we might be able to alert our child's teacher that they are feeling discouraged. Encouraging phrases to keep in mind are:
    - "I love hearing you play!"
    - "I am so proud of your dedication!"
    - "I remember when you were just beginning. Now look how far you've come!"
    - "Stick with it, and we'll ask your teacher for ideas that help."
- **Keep things positive:** Tell your child what you like about their playing and point out what is going well.

Teens can be hard on themselves, and their teacher can point out any challenges they aren't seeing clearly. There's enough to cause stress in parent-child relationships during the teen years, and I really recommend keeping your comments about your child's music playing positive and encouraging.

- **Use humor:** It's easy for tensions to run high between parents and children during these years. It's easy for misunderstandings and tensions to creep into our practice conversations too. Using humor can keep things light and keep communication open. Avoid using humor at anyone's expense, but do lighten the mood whenever possible.

- **Show up:** Attend all the performances and events your schedule allows. If your child needs help getting new music, materials, or a repair on their instrument, show you care in a tangible way by being willing to help or coach them through how to take care of it with your help. Being there when needed, and even when it's just nice to have someone show up and cheer us on, shows our support in a tangible way. It's often more important to teens than they share.

- **Feed motivation:** Look for opportunities to build motivation: concerts, extra learning opportunities, music to listen to at home. Motivation can be built through the environment around us, and you can play a big role in creating a motivating environment at home. Having something to practice for or peers to make music with can be some of the biggest motivators at this age.

Extra Support

Extra support can sometimes be needed beyond what we or our teacher can provide. Special circumstances like this can include physical, cognitive, developmental, and even medical needs that really require professional advice and sometimes ongoing help from a specialist to navigate.

In my experience teaching, sometimes it's through music or even a combination of experiences in music lessons and school that reveal to us that we should get some additional resources involved for our children. Some school districts even provide testing and screening, or you can check with your family doctor or a medical professional.

In my teaching career, I have worked with students who were diagnosed with ADHD, anxiety, dyslexia, autism, selective mutism, speech delays, and more. If you have a trusting relationship with your teacher and are willing to share such a diagnosis, it often helps us to modify our approach.

It's especially helpful to me to hear what specialists working with a student recommend for them as accommodations in school and other learning situations. Then I can adapt and also do research within my teaching community to find the best ways to tailor my lessons and assignments to the needs of your child.

I want to share a teacher and parent perspective with you that illustrates one parent's journey. It's important to remember that each student's needs are individual, even with a similar diagnosis, and this is one family's story that I hope illustrates how powerful it is to work with our child's unique needs, whatever they may be.

Suzuki teacher Kristina Turner shared her experience as a practice partner with her son who was diagnosed with autism at four years old. They first tried lessons around the time of his diagnosis for a short while but put things on pause soon after when it was hard to make things work and fit into the typical mold of how everyone else around them was doing things. Looking back, Kristina says she wished she had been more open with their teacher, who she now knows would have been very open to working with them to make lessons work for her son.

When her son was nine, and she knew he would be joining fifth-grade strings in school the following year, she resolved to try again. "By that time, I'd had a few more years of teaching and a few more years of training, and I had new language. And so I said, 'Okay, we're going to do this thing!'"

This time in practice, Kristina gave clear, not abstract, instructions. She told her son how many repetitions they would do, and they counted items, like beads, to keep track. She made it very clear when they would be done for the day, and stuck with it. Her husband remarked right away at how much connection was happening between them during practice and offered to help with other parts of the schedule so Kristina was freed up to practice with her son each day.

She shared this insight:

> Something that can really help our parents when we have students who need some extra support, or actually any kids, is having a clear structure.

> We might have to figure out what works for each student. For example, another thing that I learned about my son is he is a completionist. We were practicing "Twinkle, Twinkle, Little Star" and I said that when we had practiced ten Twinkles, we'd go up to the corner store and get a candy bar.
>
> I was expecting that we would do a couple of them that day and we'd do a couple of them the next day, and so on. But no, we had to do all ten of them right then and there. He was not going to leave his room until he finished all ten of those Twinkles so we could go to the corner store.
>
> This is when I learned it was probably a very good thing that I said ten and not one hundred. We would have been in that room until we finished them all.

As a teacher, and through what she learned working with her son, Kristina now emphasizes how we all think differently and to embrace and work with that reality:

> In our generation, everybody tried to make themselves fit and become that square peg. And some of us were able to do it pretty well because we're kind of just a squishy pentagon, so we could be shoved into that shape.
>
> But I think that pegboard needs to go away. Just let the child be the shape or the way that they are. Help them explore it the way that they want to explore it.

She emphasized that while we can't go through life only learning one way, if we start with the ways of learning and practicing that work for our child now, then we can use that to build our skills and confidence.

Everyone has their own way of learning, and we can think of learning our instrument like going through a canal. Some students are like kayaks and can steer and move through easily. Others are like a tanker that has to be carefully and slowly steered, or it will get stuck. Kristina says, "Over the course of time, they will get there. You may just have to ignore the fact that you scraped against the side of the canal. You're still going forward."

I love this way of thinking about how while progress may look different, even slow, forward progress is progress and we can embrace that our child may be simply making that progress in a way that looks different.

I asked Kristina what she saw as the benefit of music for her son so far. She shared how much emotional development has come from music and how much his communication skills have improved as well. She says it was through the connection, structure, opportunities, and support he had access to through music that all this could develop. She specifically mentioned the relationship he has developed with his wonderful teachers:

> It's all about the music, but it's not about the music at all. My son is getting one-on-one instruction with a supportive teacher who was totally focused on him. He was learning concrete ideas and concrete language and abstract ideas and abstract language. He was learning connection and social skills and humor. He would actually tease his teachers

and joke with them and be a little stinker, and they would laugh and he thought that was amazing.

What I love about this story is hearing the power of music in a young person's life. It's a great example of how sometimes as adults, we have to step back, regroup, and then approach learning music, or anything else, with a deeper understanding of the needs of our child. We have to believe it's possible and also respect how they need to do it to make it work for them.

If we think about all the factors we've discussed—age, learning differences, practice personalities, and so much more—you can see that each child has a slightly different combination of approaches and practice styles that will help them work best with you, the practice coach. General advice is helpful, but then we have to put it through the filter of what we know, and are learning, about our own child.

You don't have to understand how to perfectly practice or be a professional musician to help meet your child's unique needs in the practice room. Each child, at any given moment in time, has a unique combination of emotional, developmental, practice personality and musical needs to keep in mind and navigate. In the practice room, you can help by seeing challenges or even challenging behavior as an indication that one or more of these needs might need to be addressed in a more helpful way.

Many of us were not raised to think of each of these needs and how they might affect child behavior, and it may feel uncomfortable or unusual to think of it in these terms. However, as more research is done on learning and the brain, it becomes more evident that the behaviors we want to see in the practice room come from a combination of maturity, experience, support from adults, and our needs being met along the way.

There are factors outside our control as parents and caregivers, and even as students learning to practice ourselves. But the factors that we *do* have an impact on can make a huge difference, and we should absolutely strive to make a positive impact where we can. We can practice with more understanding and a more complete picture of our child as a whole person with unique needs and help set them up to learn to the fullest of their potential.

I hope the concepts from this book, along with guidance from your teacher, will help you with ideas you can use as you support your child and their music education.

CHAPTER TWENTY-ONE

You Are on the Same Team

As practice partners, we may want practice to be fun, creative, productive, and exciting. We may also want our children to love music and learn to play and enjoy their instrument while developing their skills. Most parents I know want there to be less conflict and frustration and more progress. I hope the information in this book gives you a starting point to help facilitate practice sessions that are more positive, peaceful, and productive.

When I think about the vision I had for my own children in music, it included:

- Wanting them to develop a deep love of music for life.
- Wanting them to gain the knowledge, through practicing, how they learn and approach new challenges.
- Wanting them to appreciate many types of music.
- Wanting them to have some of the learning and social opportunities that music had given me growing up.
- Wanting them to find what they were uniquely gifted at and what they excelled at.

These are the goals that kept me going, and I encourage you to take time to reflect on your goals for giving the gift of music to your own children as you implement the ideas in this book. Like mine, your goals and hopes for music study may include musical and non-musical outcomes. Like Kristina Turner said, "It's all about the music and it's not about the music at all."

As you close the pages of this book and go into the daily work of supporting practice, here is what I want everyone to remember:

You are on the same team as your child, working together to accomplish a goal.

It is not our job to make our children into someone they are not or to fit into a mode of learning that doesn't work for them. Working with our children in the practice room, or supporting them as they practice on their own, is an opportunity to see where their strengths lie and where they need support.

What used to be treated as character qualities and "good" behaviors in children is now understood to be a matter of learning to regulate emotions and consider what is appropriate for our child's physical, emotional, and brain development. We can encourage excellence and hard work and at the same time allow for human beings to show up in the practice room and learn together how to make music, play our instrument, and focus.

The good news is that allows *us* to be human too.

Challenging practice days will happen. Hopefully joyful, exciting days will too. Understanding what ups and downs to expect, how practice can be carefully crafted to help students navigate practice sessions, and how to work with our child's needs so they can build on them and develop a well-rounded approach over time, that works for them, is key.

Our child is responsible for the work of practice, but we can have a huge impact on helping them and setting up an environment that fosters success and learning.

I hope this book has given you many tools to do just that.

It's now time to practice.

Acknowledgments

I COULD NOT WRITE A BOOK LIKE THIS WITHOUT A HUGE SUPPORT team. I want to thank every one of you who shared ideas, gave feedback, listened, or commented as I fleshed out the ideas in this book. I specifically want to thank the following people:

A huge thank-you to my editor Shayla Raquel. You always make me sound better, help me improve my writing, and are a delight to work with.

Thank you to designer Melinda Martin for always making my books look amazing inside and out. I'm so glad to have worked with you again on this project.

Thank you to Susan Beth Barak for your help as a first reader. Your feedback was invaluable, and I know this is a better book because of your input and eye for detail. You are amazing, and I'm so grateful for your work on this project.

Thank you to Samantha Wilson, Ángel Falú-García, and Emma Pease Byron for your feedback along the way while this was in its truly rough, rough draft stages.

Thank you to all the parents, practice partners, and teachers who are a part of my music community and who gave their input and support along the way, including Dr. Molly Gebrian, Abigail Peterson, Dr. Karin Hendricks, Calida Jones, Claire Allen, Jo-Anne Steggall, Alan Duncan, Ainslie Jackel, Tayva Singer, Nitin Bhojraj, Rebecca Lane, Kimberley Wong, Tiana Angus, Billie Rose Robles,

Kristina Turner, Dr. Rebekah Hanson, Laura Sinclair, Rachel Ludt, Stephanie Bramble Chevalier, Daniela Gongora, Emily Hawe, and the whole Suzuki Triangle Community.

Thank you to my writing mentors Jeff Goins, Honoree Cordor, and Becca Syme, who each in their own way are a big reason this book even exists.

Thank you to my own parents for all of their practice with me in my young musician years and to all my teachers who guided me along the way.

Thank you to my daughters for letting me share our story about learning music and for teaching me so much about parenting. We've been through a lot together, and I think you are both amazing humans. I couldn't be prouder.

A special thank-you to my high school orchestra teacher Sr. John Therese Miller, who later became a mentor to me in my early teaching days. You taught me so much about maintaining high standards and expectations while teaching with great warmth, love, and respect for your students. I will forever be a better teacher because of you.

And finally, a huge thank-you to my husband Mike, who read every word of this book as it took shape, gave helpful feedback, and supported me through the process of writing a book during a pandemic. There aren't words to describe what your support means to me. Thank you.

Beyond the Music Lesson:
Habits of Successful Suzuki Families

USING EXCLUSIVE INTERVIEWS, CURRENT RESEARCH, AND CHRISTINE E. Goodner's own experience as a student, parent, and teacher, *Beyond the Music Lesson* gives practical advice, specific ideas, and big-picture concepts sure to help every parent who reads it.

Whether you are just beginning music lessons with your child or are an experienced parent looking for extra ideas and support, *Beyond the Music Lesson* will inspire you with new insight, motivation, and ways to make the process more successful in your own family.

This title is also available in Spanish.

Read now: https://suzukitriangle.com/books.

ABOUT THE AUTHOR

Christine E. Goodner

CHRISTINE E. GOODNER IS A DYNAMIC AND EXPERIENCED VIOLIN and early childhood music teacher with over 20 years of experience in music education. Her unique blend of expertise in music, child development, and leadership gives her a holistic approach to working with teachers, students, and their families. Christine holds a degree in early childhood education and has extensive teacher training through the Suzuki Association of the Americas (SAA). She holds a certification as a Circle of Security Parenting facilitator and is a frequent speaker and clinician around North America on the topic of supporting young music students with practice. Christine currently teaches in her studio in Hillsboro, Oregon, and is codirector of the Oregon Suzuki Institute. She is the author of *Beyond the Music Lesson: Habits of Successful Suzuki Families* (available in Spanish) and *Positive Practice: 5 Steps to Help Your Child Develop a Love of Music.* Christine hosts the *Time to Practice* podcast, which you can find along with her other resources at SuzukiTriangle.com.

Connect with the Author

Instagram.com/SuzukiTriangle
Facebook.com/ChristineEGoodner

Leave a Review

If you enjoyed *Music Practice Makeover,*
will you consider writing a review on your platform of choice?
Reviews help indie authors find more readers like you.

Notes

Chapter One: Productive and Positive Practice

[1] Seth Godin, *The Practice: Shipping Creative Work* (New York: Portfolio, 2020), p. 246.

[2] Marilee Sprenger, *Social Emotional Learning and the Brain: Strategies to Help Your Students Thrive* (Alexandria, VA: ASCD, 2020), p. 42–43.

[3] Benjamin Hardy, *Willpower Doesn't Work: Discover the Hidden Keys to Success* (New York: Hachette Books, 2018), p. 7.

[4] James Clear, *Atomic Habits: An Easy & Proven Way to Build Good Habits & Break Bad Ones* (New York: Avery, 2018), p. 191.

Chapter Three: Supporting Music Practice at Home

[1] University of Wisconsin Stevens Points, International Research Symposium on Talent Education, accessed September 13, 2021, https://www.uwsp.edu/suzuki/Pages/IRSTE/home.aspx.

Chapter Four: Real Talk about Practice

[1] William Stixrud, PhD, and Ned Johnson, *The Self-Driven Child: The Science and Sense of Giving Your Kids More Control Over Their Lives* ((New York: Penguin Random House, 2019), p. 16, 23.

Chapter Five: The True Story of What It's Like to Practice at Home with Young Children

[1] Dr. Stuart Shanker, *Self-Reg: How to Help Your Child (and You) Break the Stress Cycle and Successfully Engage with Life* (New York: Penguin Random House, 2016), p. 40.

Chapter Six: Building Great Habits from the Start

[1] US Department of State, Foreign Language Training, accessed September 13, 2021, https://www.state.gov/foreign-language-training.
[2] Christine E. Goodner, *The Suzuki Triangle Blog*, "The Reals Ups and Downs of Parent-Child Practice," June 13, 2018, https://suzukitriangle.com/the-real-life-ups-and-downs-of-parent-child-practice.

Chapter Seven: A New Way to Look at the Practice Relationship

[1] Brittany P. Gardner, *This Will Help You Grow: Advice and Encouragement for Suzuki Parents* (Self-Published, 2020), p. 21.
[2] Marilee Sprenger, p. 102.
[3] Marilee Sprenger, p. 86.
[4] Dr. Stuart Shanker, p. 26–27.
[5] Kent Hoffman, Glenn Cooper, and Bert Powell, with Christine M. Benton, *Raising a Secure Child: How Circle of Security Parenting Can Help You Nurture Your Child's Attachment, Emotional Resilience, and Freedom to Explore* (New York: The Guilford Press, 2017), p. 37.

Chapter Eight: Focus on Connection

[1] Elaine Taylor-Klaus, "How to Help with Homework: Be a Body Double," Impact Parents, accessed September 13, 2021, https://impactparents.com/blog/adhd/how-to-help-with-homework-be-a-body-double.

Chapter Nine: A Belief That Our Child Can Learn and Improve

[1] Marilee Sprenger, p. 82.
[2] Carol S. Dweck, PhD, *Mindset: The New Psychology of Success* (New York: Ballantine Books, 2016).
[3] Angela Duckworth, *Grit: The Power of Passion and Perseverance* (New York: Scribner, 2016), p. 141–142.
[4] James Clear, p. 15.

[5] Daniel Coyle, *The Little Book of Talent: 52 Tips for Improving Your Skills* (New York: Bantam, 2012), p. 13.

Chapter Twelve: Planning Changes Everything

[1] Barbara Lourie Sand, *Teaching Genius: Dorothy DeLay and the Making of a Musician* (Portland, OR: Amadeus Press, 2000), p. 53.

Chapter Thirteen: Getting Practice Started

[1] Daniel J. Siegel and Tina Payne Bryson, *The Whole-Brain Child: 12 Revolutionary Strategies to Nurture Your Child's Developing Mind* (New York: Delacorte Press, 2011), p. 24.
[2] Katherine Martinelli, "Why Do Kids Have Trouble With Transitions?" Child Mind Institute, accessed Septmeber 13, 2021, https://childmind.org/article/why-do-kids-have-trouble-with-transitions.

Chapter Fifteen: Productive Ways to Give Feedback

[1] Edmund Sprunger, *Helping Parents Practice: Ideas for Making It Easier* (St. Louis, MO: Yes Publishing, 2004), p. 16.
[2] Harold S. Koplewicz, *The Scaffold Effect: Raising Resilient, Self-Reliant, and Secure Kids in an Age of Anxiety* (New York: Harmony Books, 2021), p. 7.
[3] Doug Lemov, Erica Woolway, and Katie Yezzi, *Practice Perfect: 2 Rules for Getting Better at Getting Better* (San Francisco, CA: Jossey-Bass, 2012).

Chapter Sixteen: Ending with the Beginning in Mind

[1] Gretchen Rubin, "11 Happiness Paradoxes to Contemplate As You Think About Your Happiness Project," March 23, 2011, https://gretchenrubin.com/2011/03/11-happiness-paradoxes-to-contemplate-as-you-think-about-your-happiness-project.
[2] Marilee Sprenger, p. 106.

Chapter Seventeen: Reflecting on Results in Practice

[1] "Life Lessons: 3 Questions for Hilary Hahn," The Strad, February 7, 2019, https://www.thestrad.com/artists/-life-lessons-3-questions-for-hilary-hahn/8626.article.

[2] Dan Sullivan, "The Gap and the Gain," Strategic Couch, 2017, https://pardot-resources.s3.amazonaws.com/download/DanBook/GapAndGain/GapAndGain.pdf.

[3] Benjamin Hardy, "Unsuccessful People Focus On 'The Gap.' Here's What Successful People Focus On," accessed August 1, 2021, https://benjaminhardy.com/unsuccessful-people-focus-on-the-gap-heres-what-successful-people-focus-on.

[4] *Creative Pep Talk Podcast*, "Sick of Your Own Work? How to Make Work You Love Again in 5 Steps," Episode 317, https://www.creativepeptalk.com/episodes/317.

Chapter Eighteen: Build a Practice Toolkit

[1] Marilee Sprenger, p. 106–107.

[2] Marilee Sprenger, p. 197.

[3] Dr. Daniel Siegel and Dr. Tina Payne Bryson, p. 59.

[4] "Parents Should Know They're Not Alone: An Interview With Kimberley Wong," *Time to Practice Podcast*, suzukitriangle.com/ttpepisode2.

Made in United States
Troutdale, OR
09/12/2023

12841366R00152